Geography Workbook
Cycle Three

The Americas & the 50 United States of America

Acknowledgments

A debt of gratitude goes to Doris Dean and J. Bruce Jones for producing our Cycle 3 Aquinas Learning Geography Curriculum. Thank you for sharing your time and talents with all of us! ~Rosario Reilly, President, Aquinas Learning, LLC.

Geography: The Americas & the 50 United States of America
Aquinas Learning Geography Program – Cycle 3

© Copyright Aquinas Learning LLC 2014
Map Illustrations © Copyright Bruce Jones Design 2014

Our Duplicating/Copying Policy:

All rights reserved.

No part of this book may be reproduced, stored in a retrieval system, or transmitted in any form or by any means, electronic, mechanical, photocopying, recording, or otherwise, without the prior written permission of the author, except as provided by the USA copyright law and the specific policy below:

The blank outline maps in this handbook may be freely printed and copied by a mentor or parent for use in a classroom or in the homeschool. The labeled maps may not be copied.

Aquinas Learning LLC
P.O. Box 253
Manassas, VA 20108
www.AquinasLearning.com

Geography

The Americas & the 50 United States of America

List of Maps

Regional Maps	Page
World-Robinson Projection	2
North America	4
Canada	6
United States of America	8
Central America	10
South America	12

State by Admission to the Union	Page
Delaware	14
Pennsylvania	16
New Jersey	18
Georgia	20
Connecticut	22
Massachusetts	24
Maryland	26
South Carolina	28
New Hampshire	30
Virginia	32
New York	34
North Carolina	36
Rhode Island	38
Vermont	40
Kentucky	42
Tennessee	44
Ohio	46
Louisiana	48
Indiana	50
Mississippi	52
Illinois	54
Alabama	56
Maine	58

State by Admission to the Union	Page
Missouri	60
Arkansas	62
Michigan	64
Florida	66
Texas	68
Iowa	70
Wisconsin	72
California	74
Minnesota	76
Oregon	78
Kansas	80
West Virginia	82
Nevada	84
Nebraska	86
Colorado	88
North Dakota	90
South Dakota	92
Montana	94
Washington	96
Idaho	98
Wyoming	100
Utah	102
Oklahoma	104
New Mexico	106
Arizona	108
Alaska	110
Hawaii	112

Territories	Page
Guam, Saipan, Northern Mariana Islands	114
Puerto Rico	116
United States Virgin Islands	118

Aquinas Learning LLC

Geography

The Americas & the 50 United States of America

Alpha List of Maps

Regional Maps	Page
Canada	6
Central America	10
North America	4
South America	12
United States of America	8
World-Robinson Projection	2

States and Territories	Page
Alabama	56
Alaska	110
Arizona	108
Arkansas	62
California	74
Colorado	88
Connecticut	22
Delaware	14
Florida	66
Georgia	20
Guam	114
Hawaii	112
Idaho	98
Illinois	54
Indiana	50
Iowa	70
Kansas	80
Kentucky	42
Louisiana	48
Maine	58
Maryland	26
Massachusetts	24
Michigan	64

States and Territories	Page
Minnesota	76
Mississippi	52
Missouri	60
Montana	94
Nebraska	86
Nevada	84
New Hampshire	30
New Jersey	18
New Mexico	106
New York	34
North Carolina	36
North Dakota	90
Northern Marianas Islands	114
Ohio	46
Oklahoma	104
Oregon	78
Pennsylvania	16
Puerto Rico	116
Rhode Island	38
Saipan	114
South Carolina	28
South Dakota	92
Tennessee	44
Texas	68
US Virgin Islands	118
Utah	102
Vermont	40
Virginia	32
Washington	96
West Virginia	82
Wisconsin	72
Wyoming	100

Aquinas Learning LLC

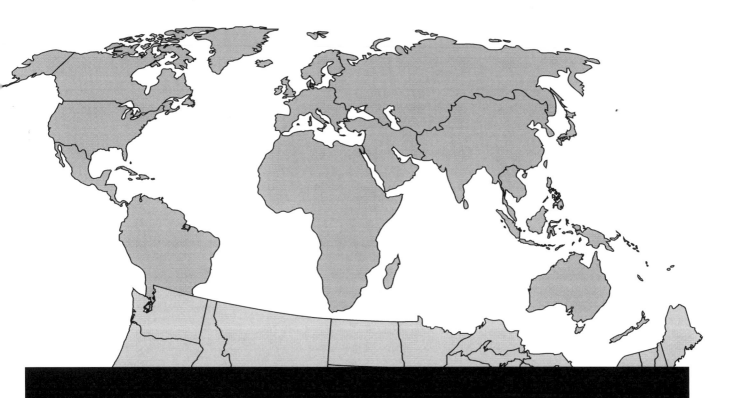

Geography Workbook
Cycle Three

The Americas & the 50 United States of America

World-Robinson Projection

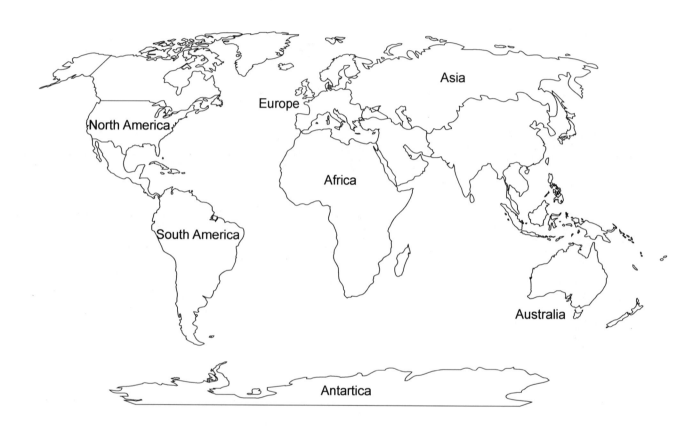

World-Robinson Projection

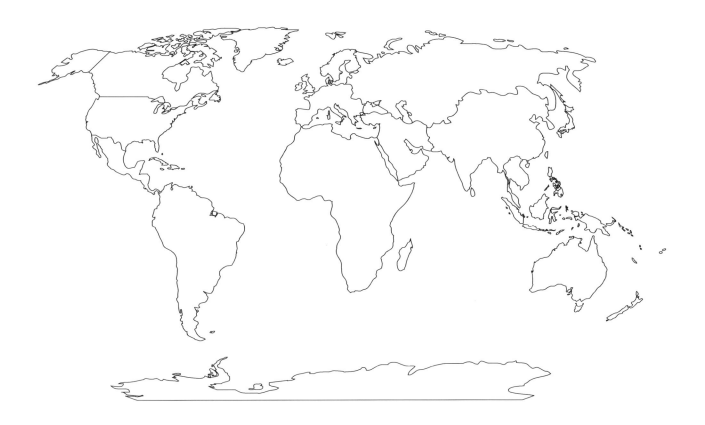

North America

North America

Canada

Canada

United States of America

United States of America

Central America

Central America

South America

South America

Delaware

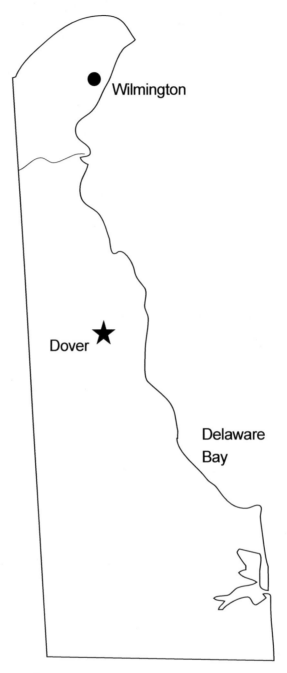

Entered the Union
December 7, 1787

Delaware

Capital: Dover
Population: 907,135
Size: 2,490 sq mi
Statehood: December 7, 1787 (1st)
Motto: Liberty and Independence
Nickname: The First State
Bird: Blue Hen Chicken
Flower: Peach Blossom
Tree: American Holly
Fun Fact: A 10 foot diameter frying pan, which could hold 180 gallons of oil and 800 chicken quarters was built in 1950 for the Delmarva Chicken Festival.

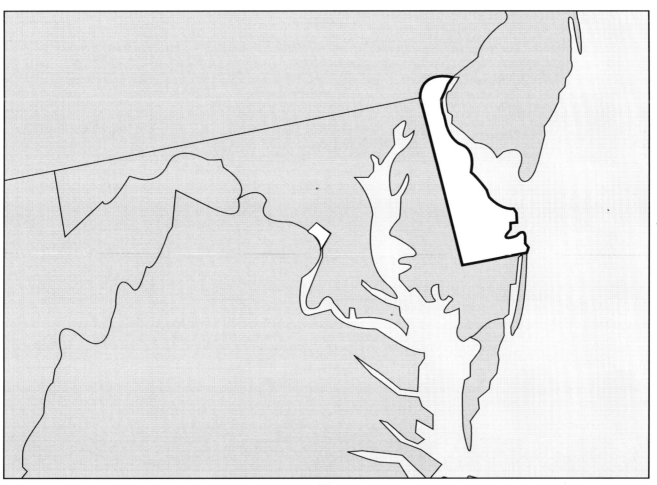

Pennsylvania

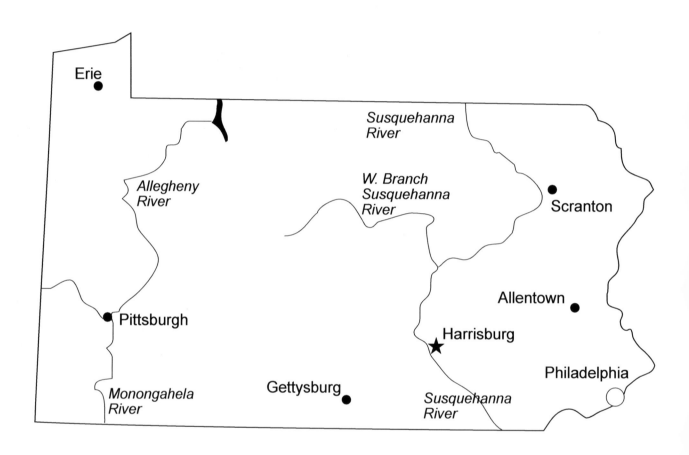

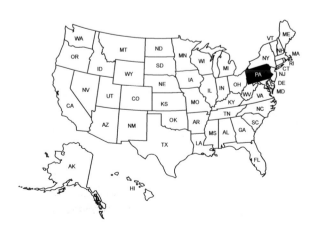

Entered the Union
December 12, 1787

Pennsylvania

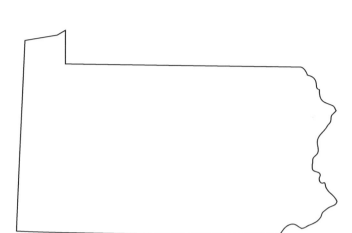

Capital: Harrisburg
Population: 12,742,886
Size: 46,055 sq mi
Statehood: December 12, 1787 (2nd)
Motto: Virtue, Liberty and Independence
Nickname: Keystone State, Quaker State
Bird: Ruffed Grouse
Flower: Mountain Laurel
Tree: Eastern Hemlock
Fun Fact: The Philadelphia Zoo is the first public zoo in the United States, founded by Benjamin Franklin.

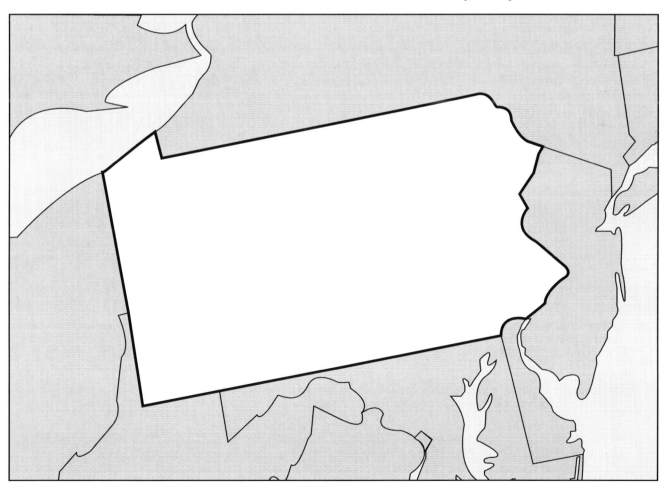

New Jersey

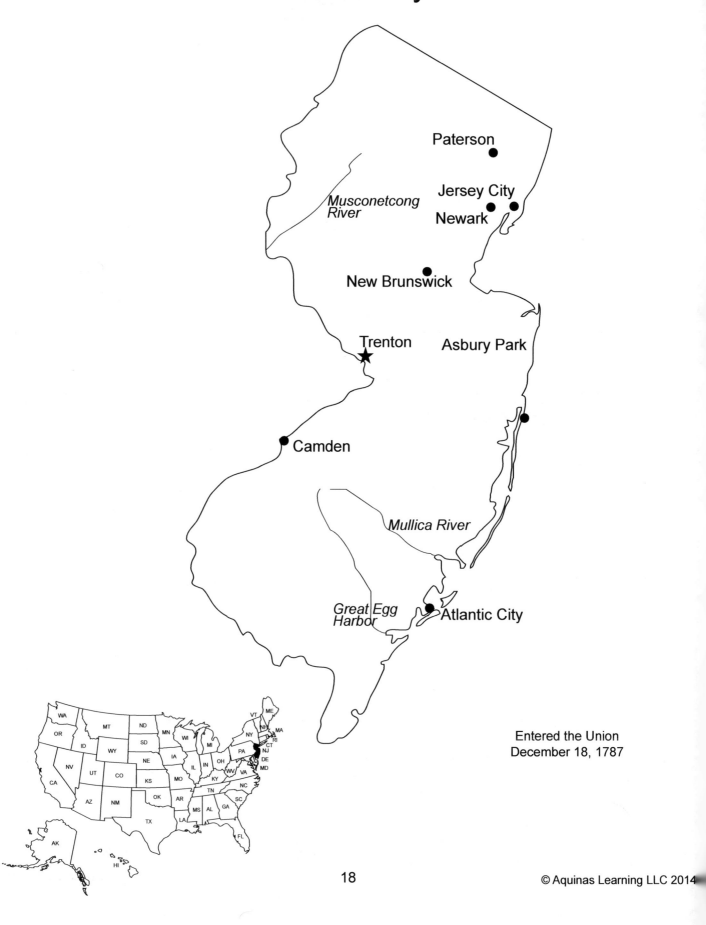

Entered the Union
December 18, 1787

New Jersey

Capital: Trenton
Population: 8,821,155
Size: 8,721 sq mi
Statehood: December 18, 1787
Motto: Liberty and Prosperity
Nickname: The Garden State
Bird: Eastern Goldfinch
Flower: Violet
Tree: Red Oak
Fun Fact: The largest spoon collection in the world is located at the Lambert Castle Museum in Paterson, New Jersey.

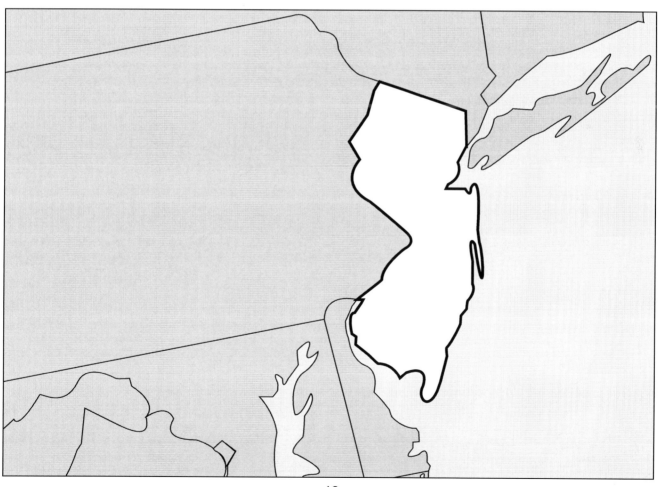

Georgia

Entered the Union
January 2, 1788

Georgia

Capital: Atlanta
Population: 9,815,210
Size: 59,425 sq mi
Statehood: January 2, 1788 (4th)
Motto: Wisdom, Justice, and Moderation
Nickname: The Peach State, The Goober State
Bird: Brown Thrasher
Flower: Cherokee Rose
Tree: Live Oak
Fun Fact: The world's largest college campus is Berry College in Rome, Georgia.

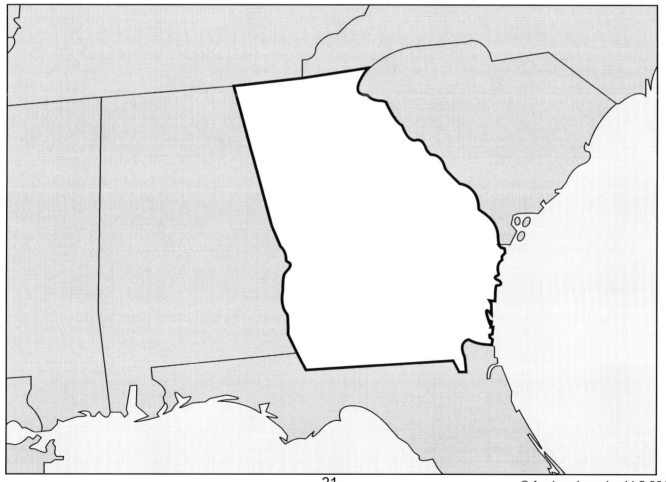

Connecticut

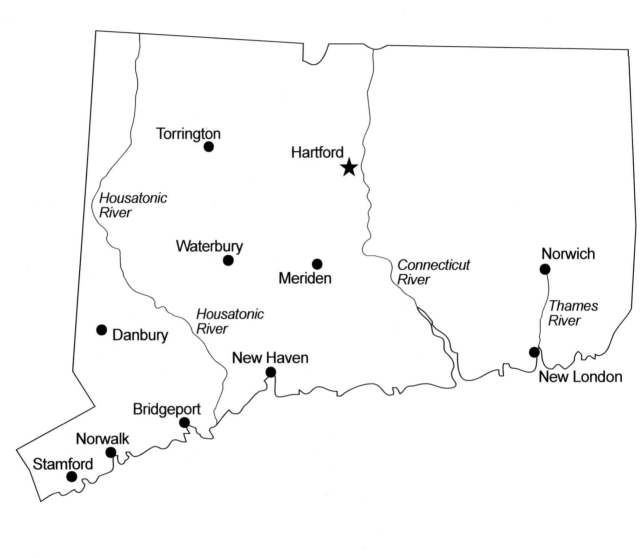

Entered the Union
January 9, 1788

Connecticut

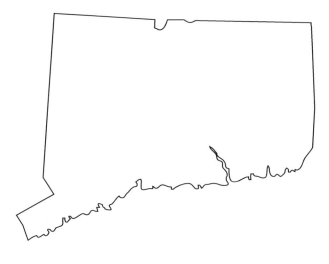

Capital: Hartford
Population: 3,580,709
Size: 5,543 sq mi
Statehood: January 9, 1788 (5th)
Motto: He Who Transplanted Still Sustains
Nickname: The Constitution State, The Nutmeg State
Bird: Robin
Flower: Mountain Laurel
Tree: White Oak
Fun Fact: The first steel mill in the United States was located in Simsbury in 1728.

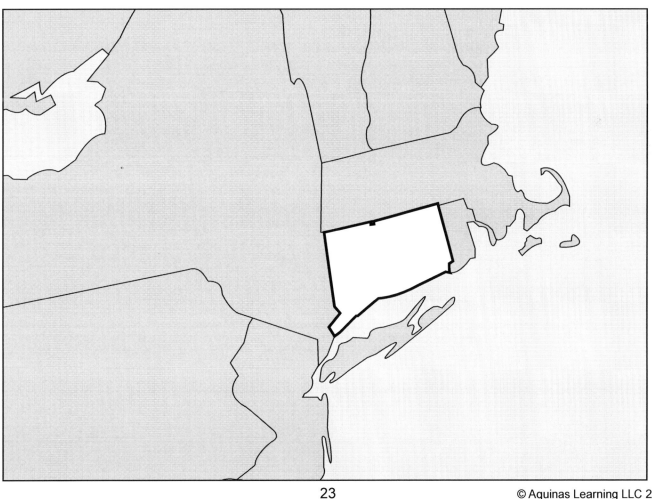

Massachusetts

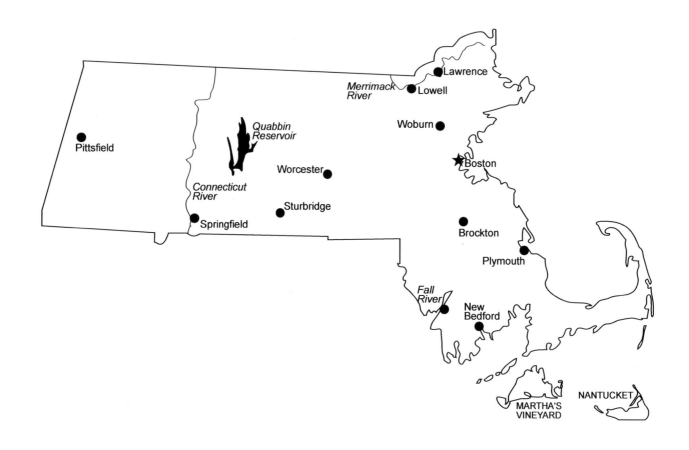

Entered the Union
February 6, 1788

Massachusetts

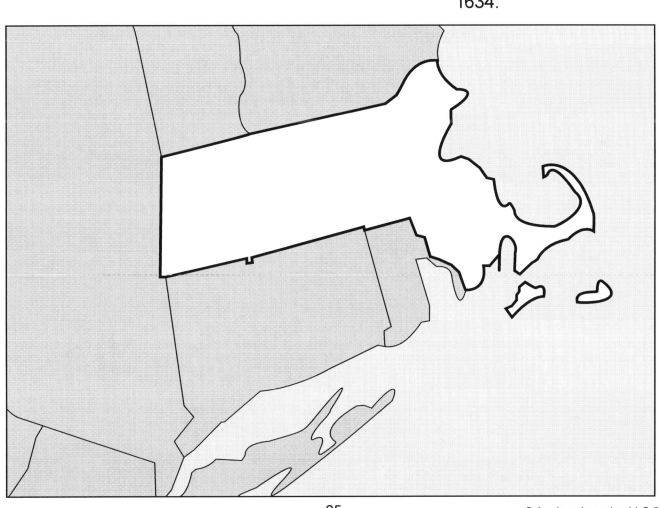

Capital: Boston
Population: 6,587,536
Size: 10,555 sq mi
Statehood: February 6, 1788 (6th)
Motto: By the Sword We Seek Peace, But Peace Only Under Liberty
Nickname: The Bay State
Bird: Black-capped Chickadee
Flower: Mayflower
Tree: American Elm
Fun Fact: The Boston Common is the first public park in America, founded in 1634.

Maryland

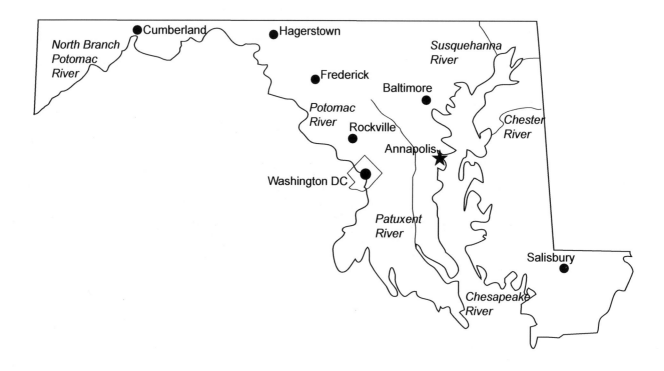

Entered the Union
April 28, 1788

Maryland

Capital:	Annapolis
Population:	5,828,289
Size:	12,407 sq mi
Statehood:	April 28, 1788 (7th)
Motto:	Manly Deeds, Womanly Words
Nickname:	Old Line State; Free State; Little America
Bird:	Baltimore Oriole
Flower:	Black-Eyed Susan
Tree:	White Oak
Fun Fact	The first school in the country opened in 1696, the King William School, in Annapolis, Maryland.

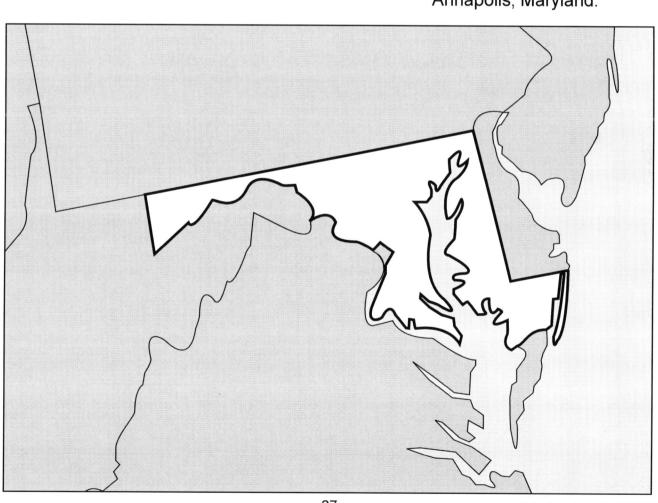

South Carolina

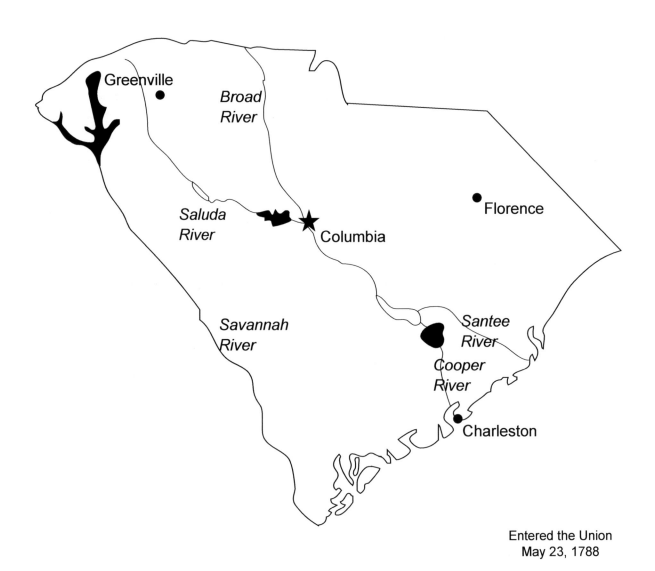

Entered the Union
May 23, 1788

South Carolina

Capital: Columbia
Population: 4,679,230
Size: 31,113 sq mi
Statehood: May 23, 1788 (8th)
Motto: While I Breathe, I Hope
Nickname: The Palmetto State
Bird: Great Carolina Wren
Flower: Yellow Jessamine
Tree: Cabbage Palmetto
Fun Fact: The oldest minor league stadium in the country is Duncan Park Baseball Stadium in Spartanburg, South Carolina.

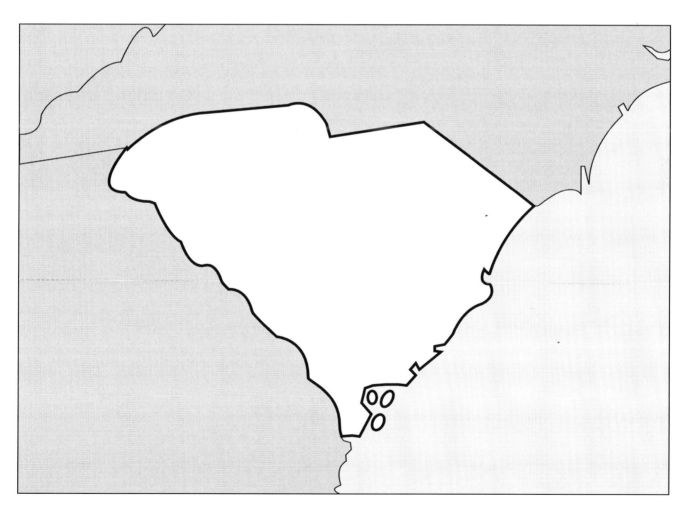

New Hampshire

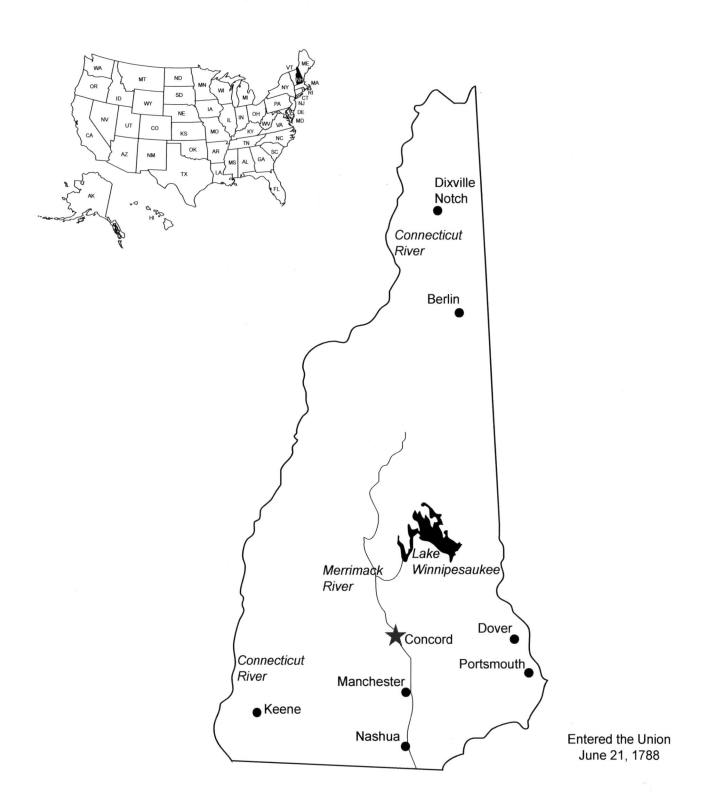

New Hampshire

Capital: Concord
Population: 1,316,470
Size: 9,304 sq mi
Statehood: June 21, 1788 (9th)
Motto: Live Free or Die
Nickname: The Granite State
Bird: Purple Finch
Flower: Purple Lilac
Tree: White Birch
Fun Fact: The first free public library was established in Peterborough in 1833.

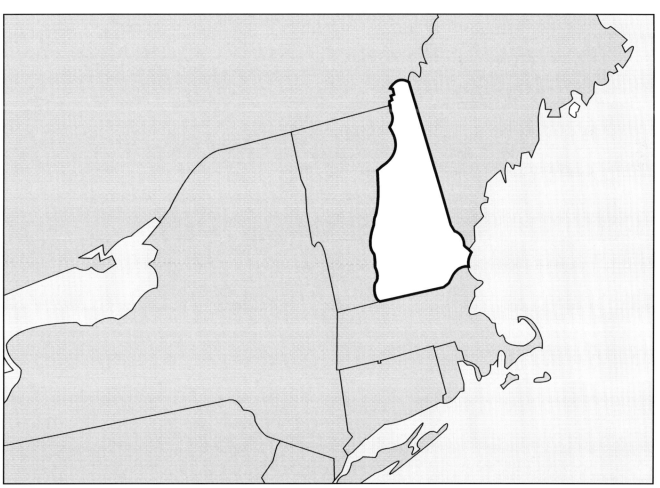

Virginia

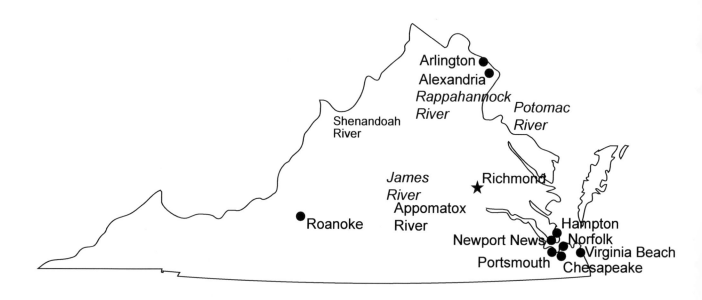

Entered the Union
June 25, 1788

Virginia

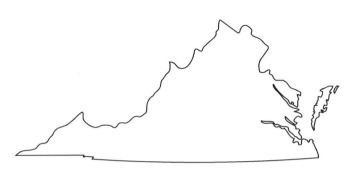

Capital: Richmond
Population: 8,096,604
Size: 42,774 sq mi
Statehood: June 25, 1788 (10th)
Motto: Thus Always to
Nickname: Old Dominion, Mother of Presidents
Bird: Cardinal
Flower: Dogwood
Tree: Dogwood
Fun Fact: The largest office building in the world is located in Arlington, Virginia, the Pentagon.

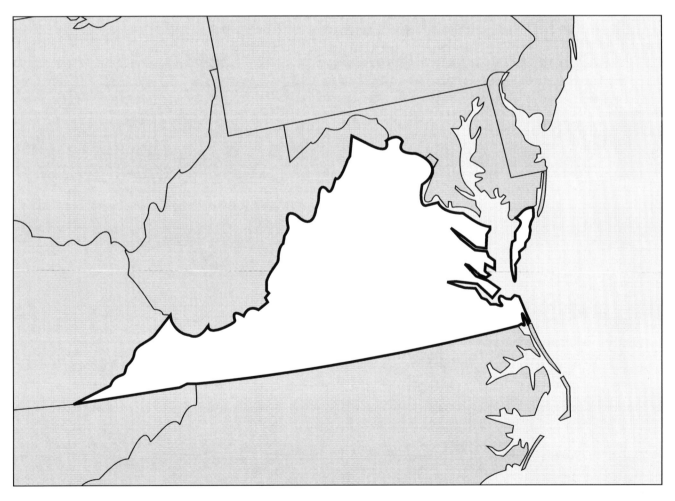

New York

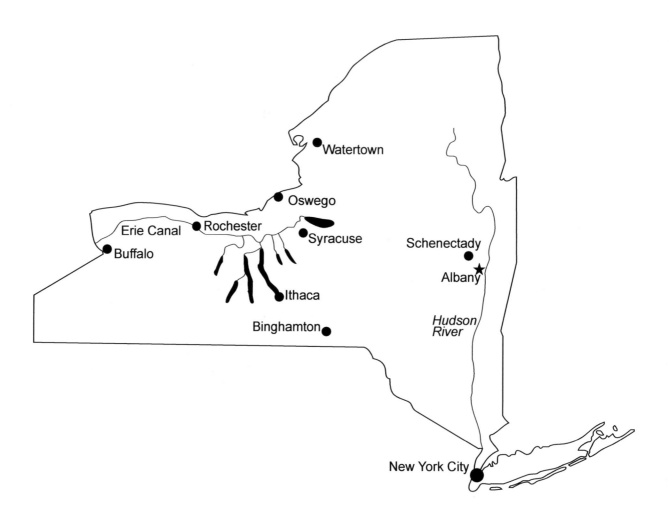

Entered the Union
July 26, 1788

New York

Capital: Albany
Population: 19,465,197
Size: 54,556 sq mi
Statehood: July 26, 1788 (11th)
Motto: Ever Upward
Nickname: The Empire State
Bird: Bluebird
Flower: Rose
Tree: Sugar Maple
Fun Fact: The oldest cattle ranch in the US is located on Montauk on Long Island, founded in 1747.

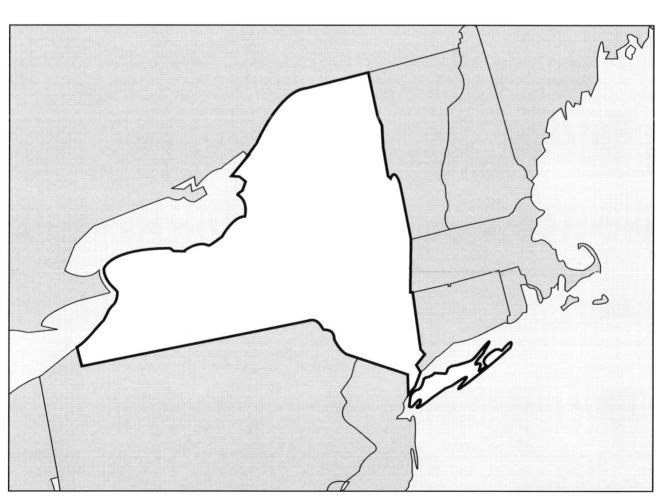

North Carolina

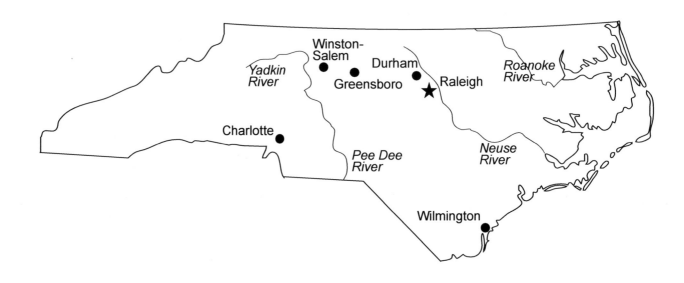

Entered the Union
November 21, 1789

North Carolina

Capital:	Raleigh
Population:	9,656,401
Size:	53,819 sq mi
Statehood:	November 21, 1789 (12th)
Motto:	First in Flight
Nickname:	Tar Heal State, The Old North State
Bird:	Cardinal
Flower:	American Dogwood
Tree:	Longleaf Pine
Fun Fact:	Fayetteville, North Carolina is the home of the first miniature golf course.

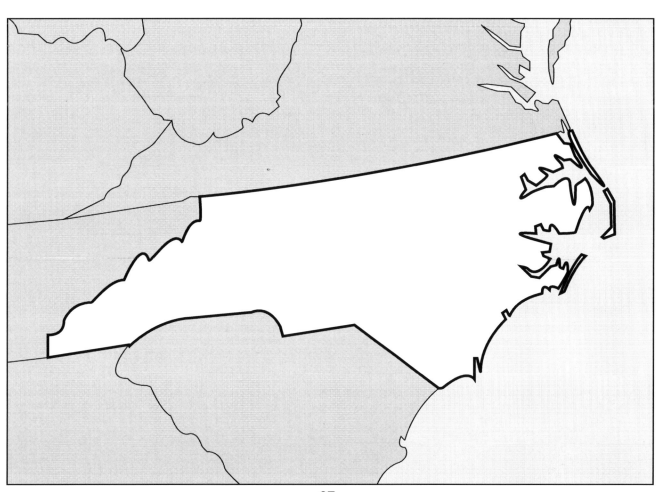

Rhode Island

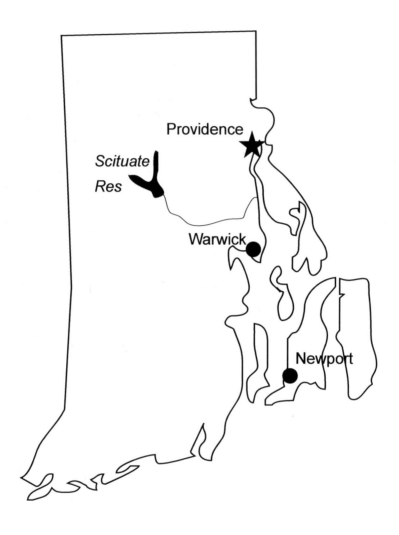

Entered the Union
May 29, 1790

Rhode Island

Capital: Providence
Population: 1, 052,567
Size: 1,214 sq mi
Statehood: May 29, 1790 (13th)
Motto: Hope
Nickname: The Ocean State
Bird: Rhode Island Red
Flower: Violet
Tree: Red Maple
Fun Fact: The larges bug in the world sits on top of the New England Pest Control building in Providence. It is a 58 foot long blue termite.

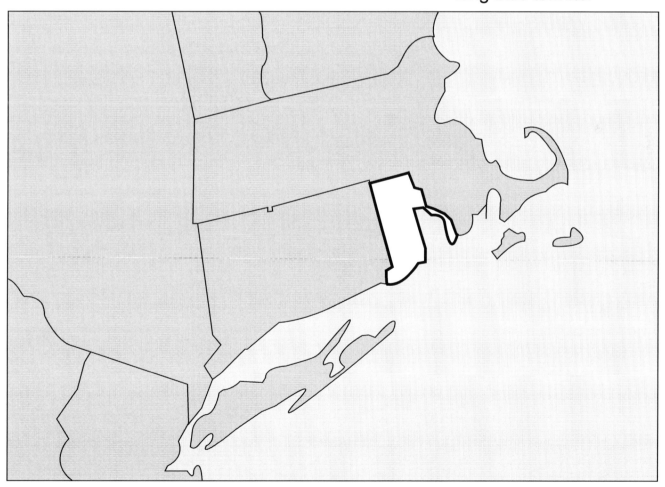

Vermont

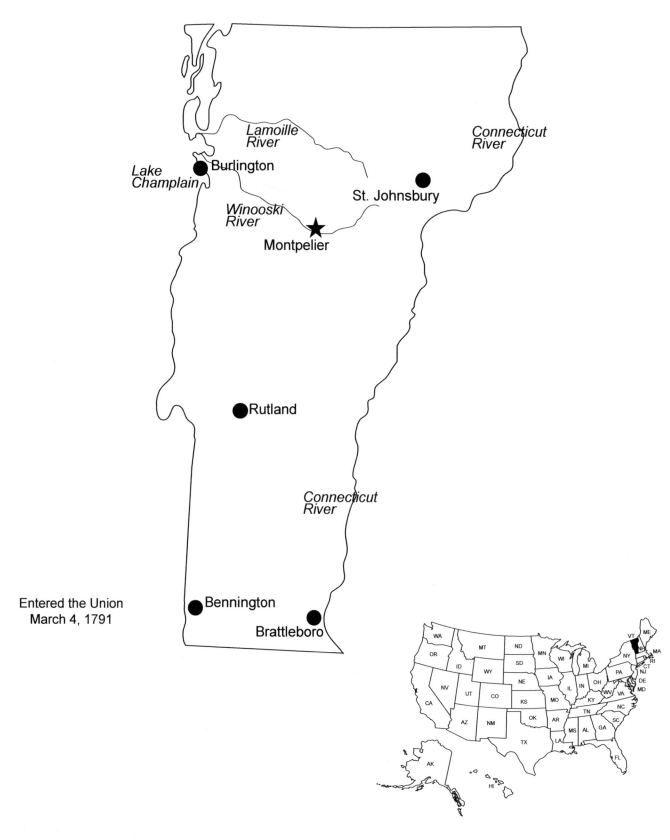

Entered the Union
March 4, 1791

Vermont

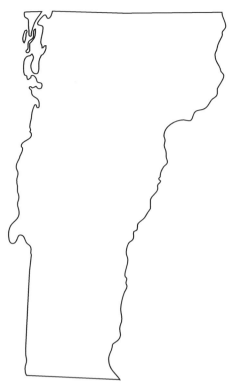

Capital: Montpelier
Population: 626,431
Size: 9,620 sq mi
Statehood: March 4, 1791 (14th)
Motto: Freedom and Unity
Nickname: The Green Mountain State
Bird: Hermit Thrush
Flower: Red Clover
Tree: Sugar Maple
Fun Fact: Montpelier is the smallest state capital in the nation, under 9,000 people.

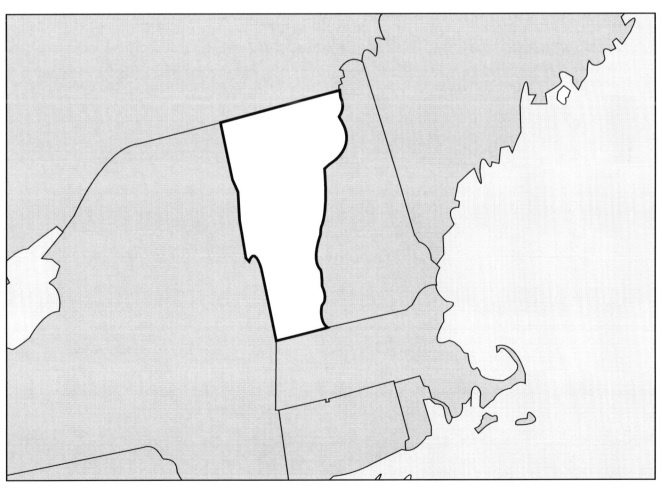

Kentucky

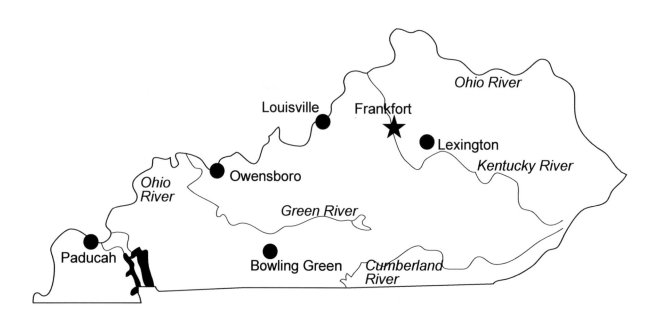

Entered the Union
June 1, 1792

Kentucky

Capital:	Frankfort
Population:	4,369,356
Size:	40,409 sq mi
Statehood:	June 1, 1792 (15th)
Motto:	United We Stand, Divided We Fall
Nickname:	The Bluegrass State
Bird:	Cardinal
Flower:	Goldenrod
Tree:	Tulip Poplar
Fun Fact:	The Kentucky Derby is the oldest continuously held horse race in the United States, starting in 1875.

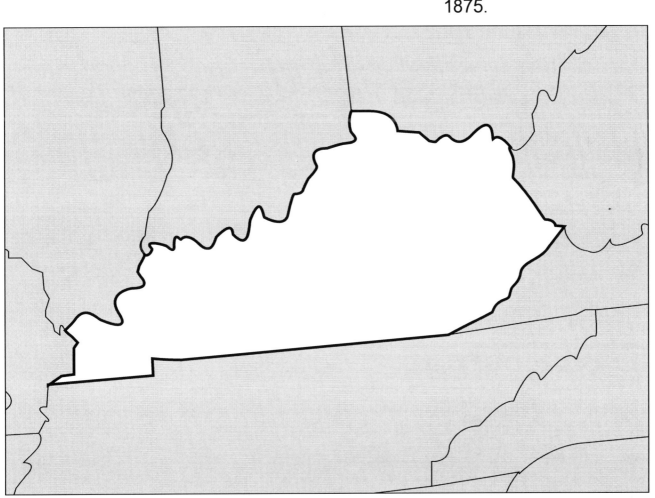

Tennessee

Entered the Union
June 1, 1796

Tennessee

Capital:	Nashville
Population:	6,403,353
Size:	42,143 sq mi
Statehood:	June 1, 1796 (16)
Motto:	Agriculture and Commerce
Nickname:	The Volunteer State
Bird:	Mockingbird
Flower:	Iris
Tree:	Tulip Poplar
Fun Fact:	Reelfoot Lake is know as the Turtle Capital of the World.

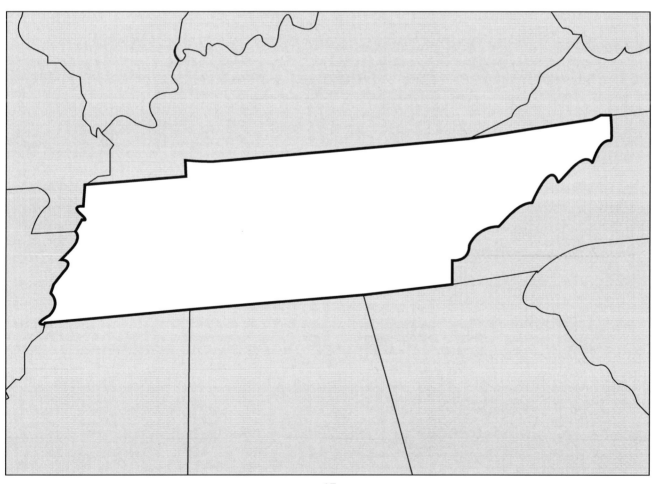

Ohio

Entered the Union
March 1, 1803

Ohio

Capital: Columbus
Population: 11,544,951
Size: 44,825 sq mi
Statehood: March 1, 1803 (17th)
Motto: With god, All Things Are Possible
Nickname: The Buckeye State, The Mother of Presidents
Bird: Cardinal
Flower: Scarlet Carnation
Tree: Buckeye
Fun Fact: The world largest basket is located at Basket Village USA in Dresden.

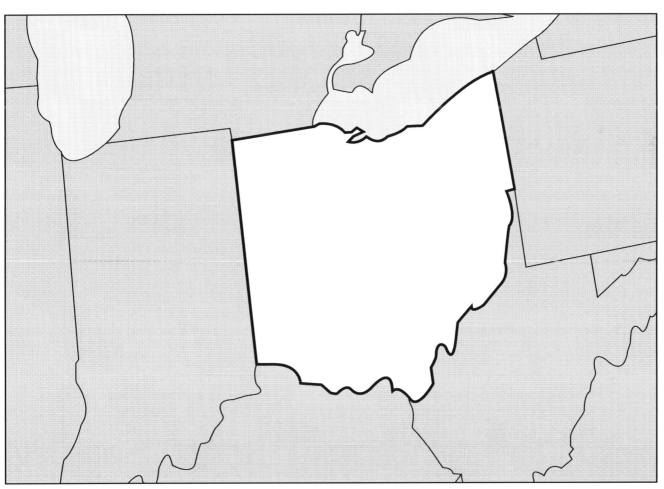

Louisiana

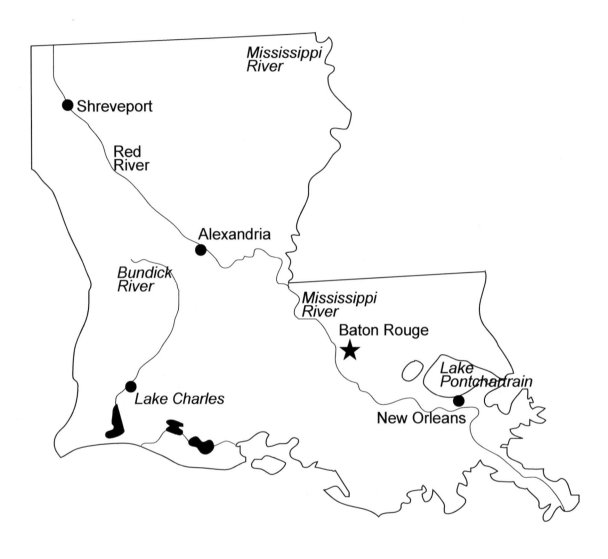

Entered the Union
April 30, 1812

Louisiana

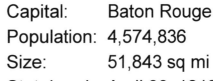

Capital: Baton Rouge
Population: 4,574,836
Size: 51,843 sq mi
Statehood: April 30, 1812 (18th)
Motto: Union, Justice and Confidence Union
Nickname: Bayou State, Pelican State
Bird: Eastern Brown Pelican
Flower: Magnolia
Tree: Bald Cypress
Fun Fact: Pirates once used the town of Jean Lafitte as a hideaway.

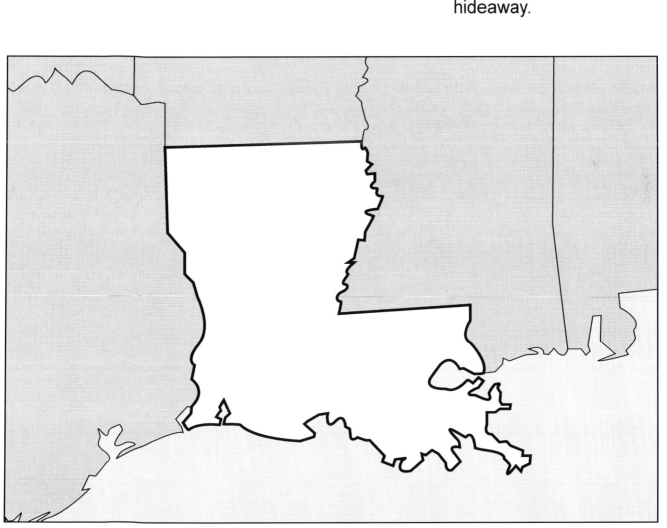

Indiana

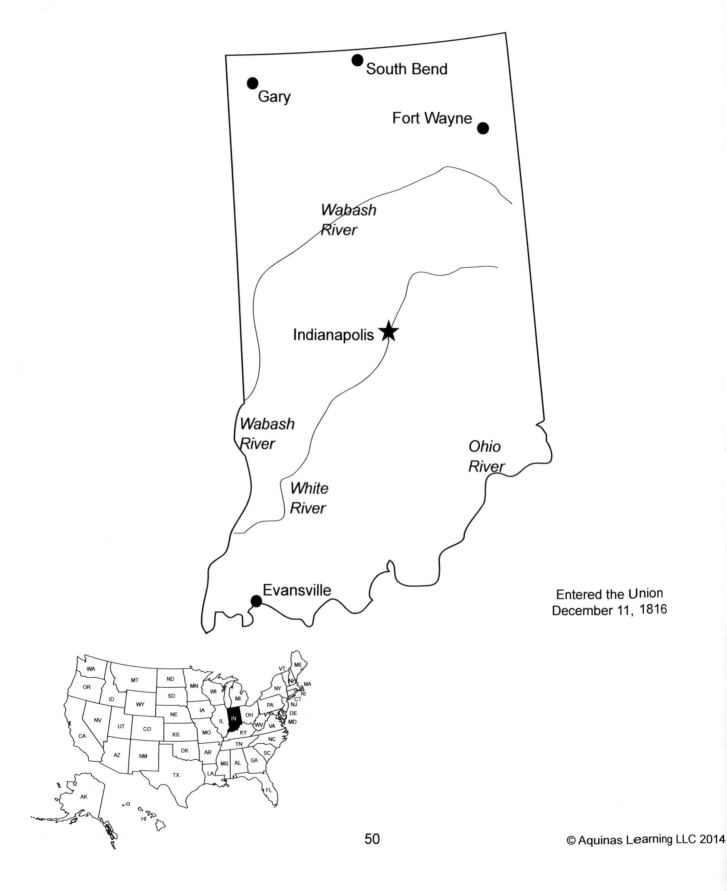

Entered the Union
December 11, 1816

Indiana

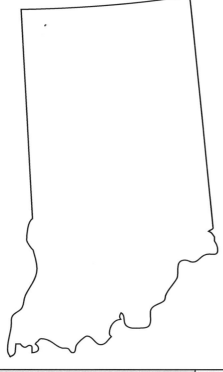

Capital: Indianapolis
Population: 6,516,922
Size: 36,418 sq mi
Statehood: December 11, 1816 (19th)
Motto: The Crossroads of America
Nickname: The Hoosier State
Bird: Cardinal
Flower: Peony
Tree: Tulip Tree
Fun Fact: The Raggedy Ann doll was created by Arcella Gruella of Indianapolis in 1914.

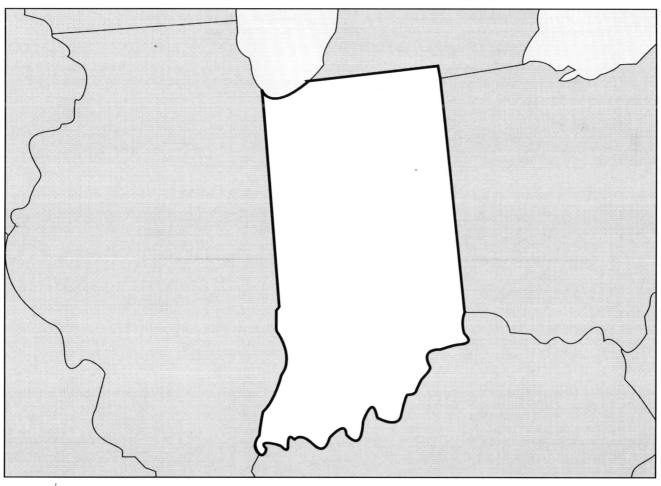

Mississippi

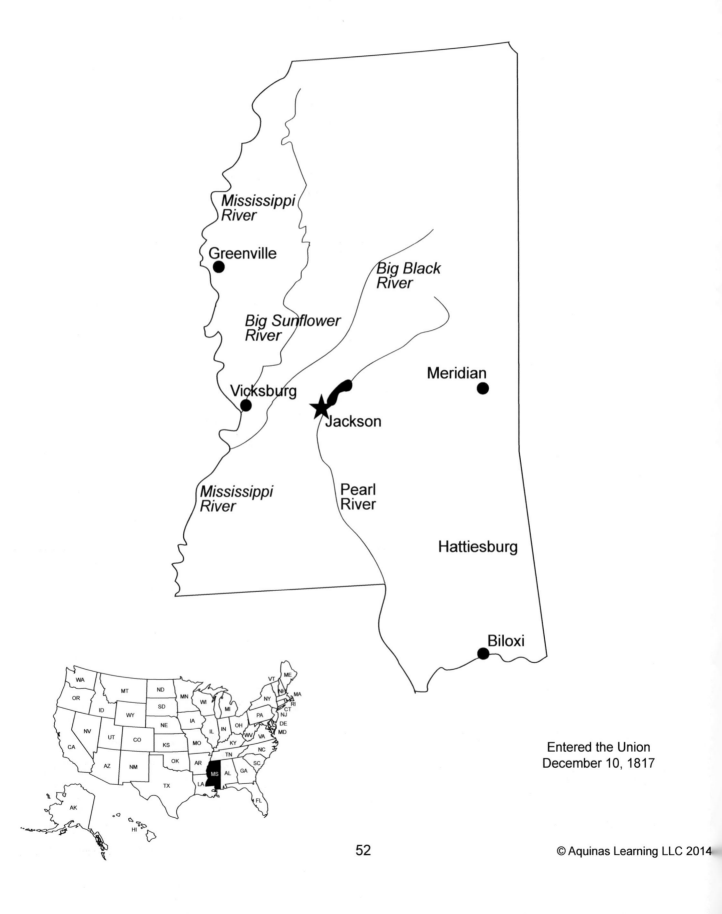

Entered the Union
December 10, 1817

Mississippi

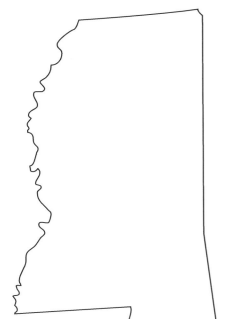

Capital: Jackson
Population: 2,978,512
Size: 48,430 sq mi
Statehood: December 10, 1817 (20th)
Motto: By Valor and Arms
Nickname: The Magnolia State
Bird: Mockingbird
Flower: Magnolia
Tree: Magnolia
Fun Fact: The Catfish Capital of the world is located in Belzoni, Mississippi.

Illinois

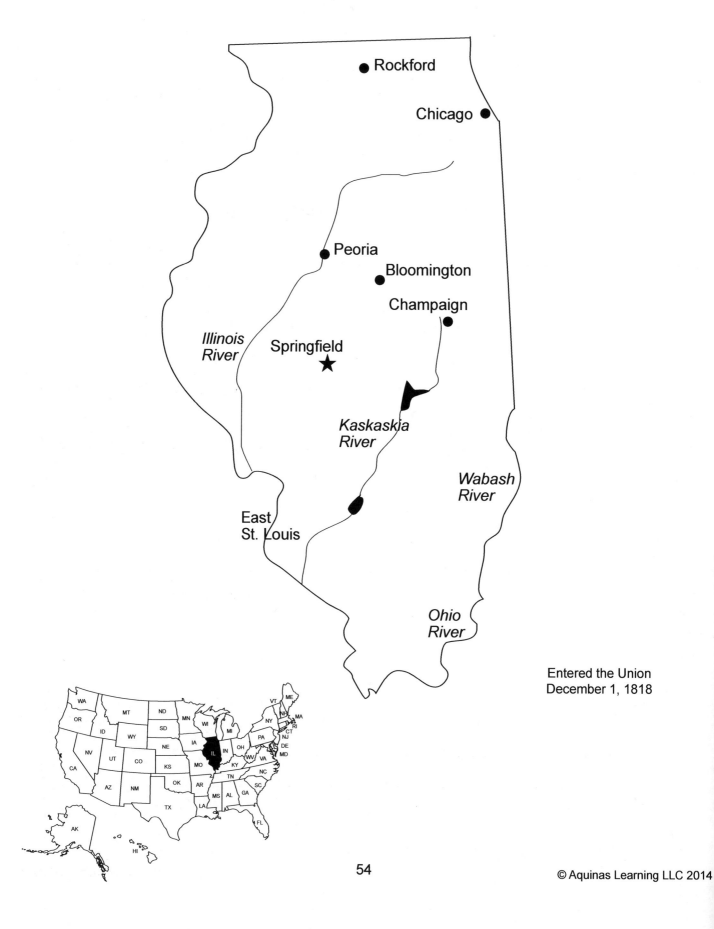

Entered the Union
December 1, 1818

Illinois

Capital:	Springfield
Population:	12,869,257
Size:	57,914 sq mi
Statehood:	December 3, 1818 (21st)
Motto:	State Sovereignty, National Union
Nickname:	The Land of Lincoln, The Prairie State
Bird:	Cardinal
Flower:	Native Violet
Tree:	White Oak
Fun Fact:	The world's largest cookie and cracker factory (Nabisco) is located in Chicago as well as the world's largest ice cream cone factory, Keebler.

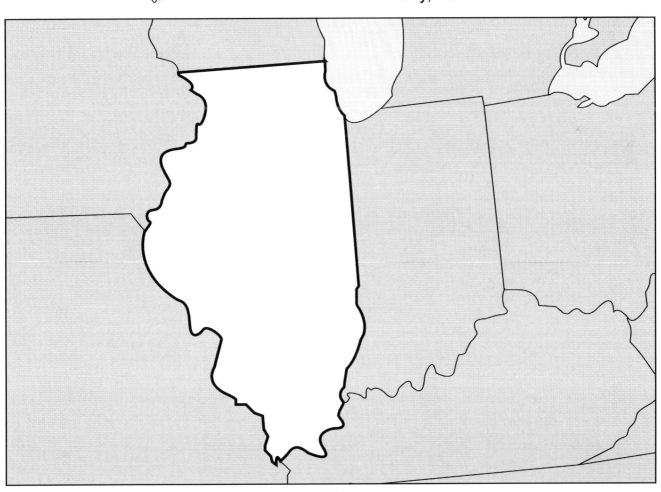

Alabama

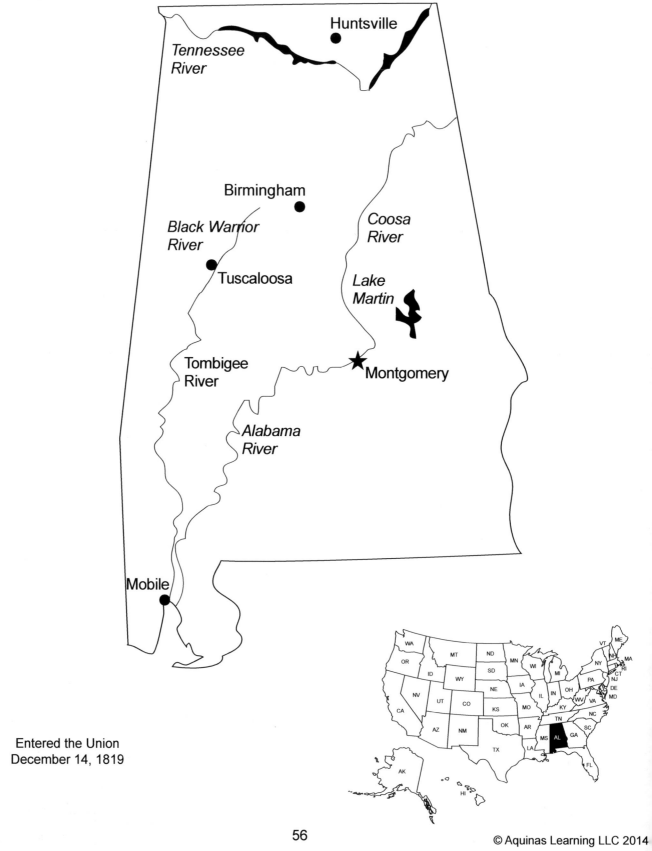

Entered the Union
December 14, 1819

Alabama

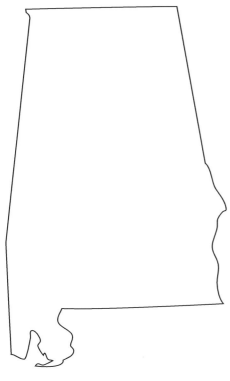

Capital: Montgomery
Population: 4,802,740
Size: 52,419 sq mi
Statehood: December 14, 1819 (22nd)
Motto: We Dare Defend Our Rights
Nickname: The Heart of Dixie, Yellowhammer State
Bird: Yellowhammer
Flower: Camellia
Tree: Southern Longleaf Pine
Fun Fact: Huntsville, Alabama is known as the rocket capital of the world.

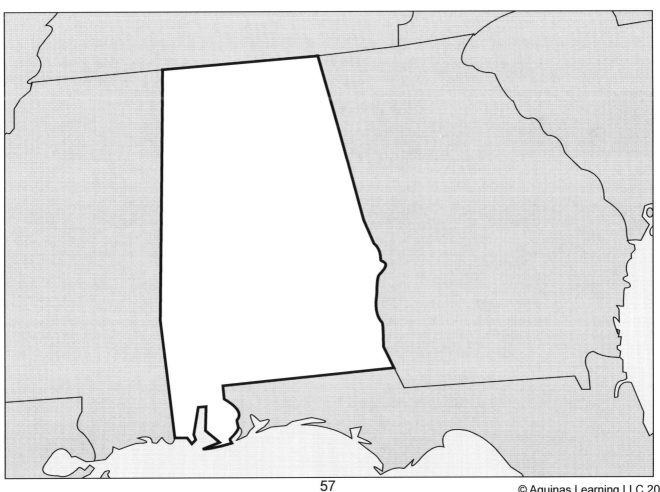

Maine

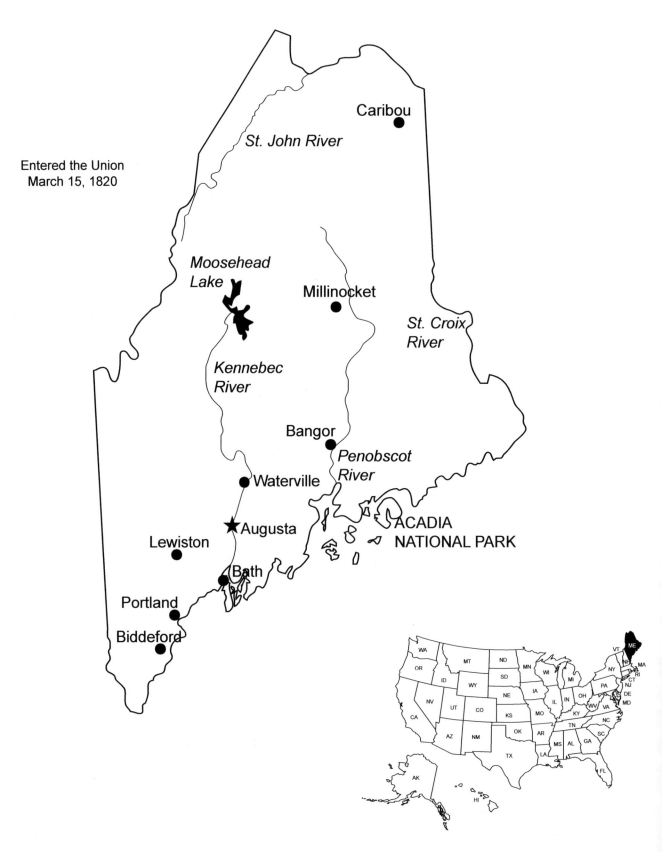

Maine

Capital: Augusta
Population: 1,328,188
Size: 35,385 sq mi
Statehood: March 15, 1820 (23rd)
Motto: I Lead
Nickname: The Pine Tree: State
Bird: Chickadee
Flower: White Pine Cone and Tassel
Tree: Eastern White Pine
Fun Fact: 90% of the US toothpick supply comes from Maine.

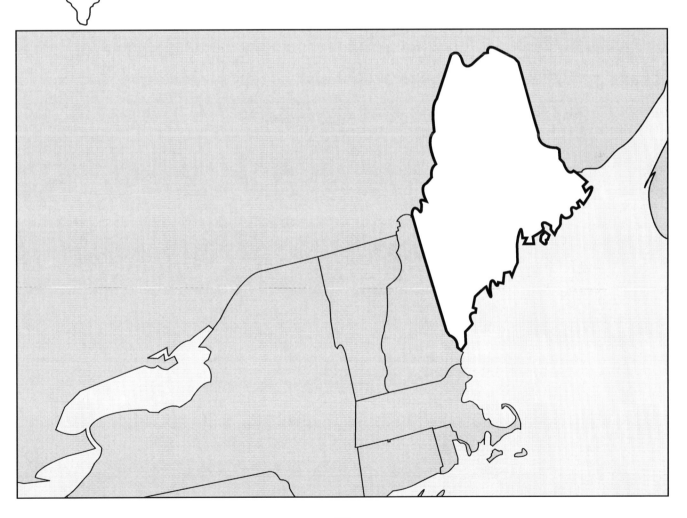

Missouri

Entered the Union
August 10, 1821

Missouri

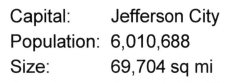

Capital: Jefferson City
Population: 6,010,688
Size: 69,704 sq mi
Statehood: August 10, 1821 (24th)
Motto: The Welfare of the People Shall Be the Supreme Law
Nickname: The Show-Me State
Bird: Bluebird
Flower: Hawthorn
Tree: American Dogwood
Fun Fact: The Anheuser-Busch brewery in St. Louis is the largest beer producing plant in the country.

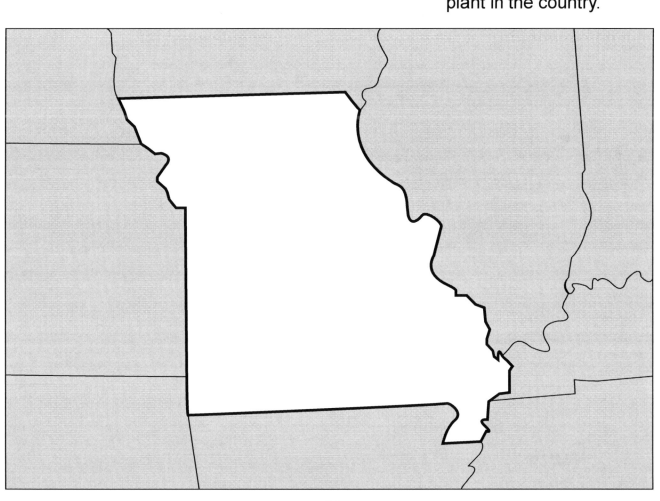

Arkansas

Entered the Union
June 15, 1836

Arkansas

Capital:	Little Rock
Population:	2,937,979
Size:	53,179 sq mi
Statehood:	June 15, 1836 (25th)
Motto:	The People Rule
Nickname:	The Natural State, The Land of Opportunity
Bird:	Mockingbird
Flower:	Apple Blossom
Tree:	Pine
Fun Fact:	Stuttgart, Arkansas holds the annual World's Championship Duck Calling Contest, originally begun in 1936 and held annually.

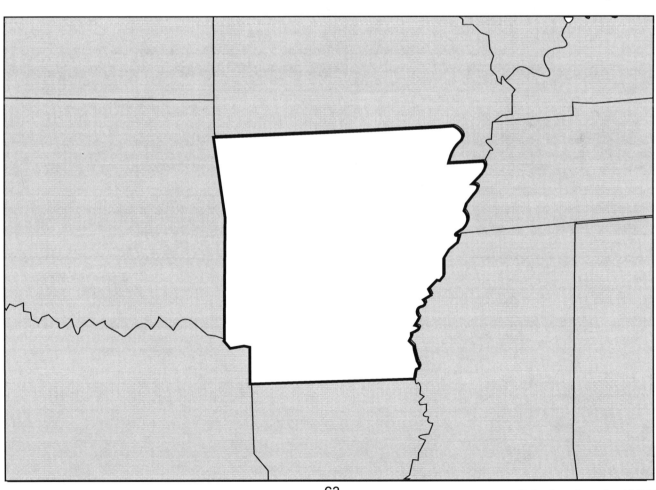

Michigan

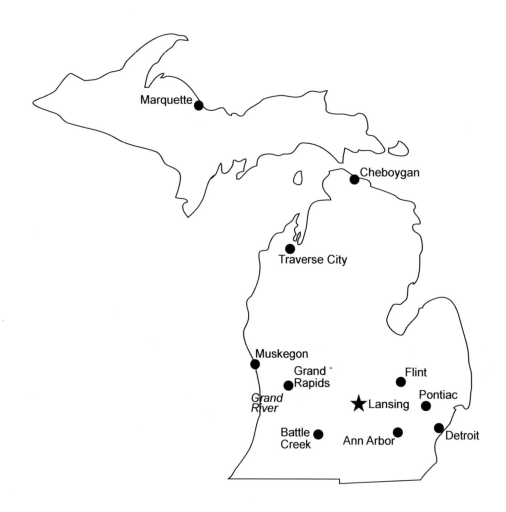

Entered the Union
January 26, 1837

Michigan

Capital:	Lansing
Population:	9,876,187
Size:	96,716 sq mi
Statehood:	January 26, 1837 (26th)
Motto:	If You Seek a Pleasant Peninsula, Look About You
Nickname:	The Great Lakes State, The Wolverine State
Bird:	Robin
Flower:	Apple Blossom
Tree:	White Pine
Fun Fact:	The largest crucifix in the world is located in Indian River and is know as the Cross in the Woods.

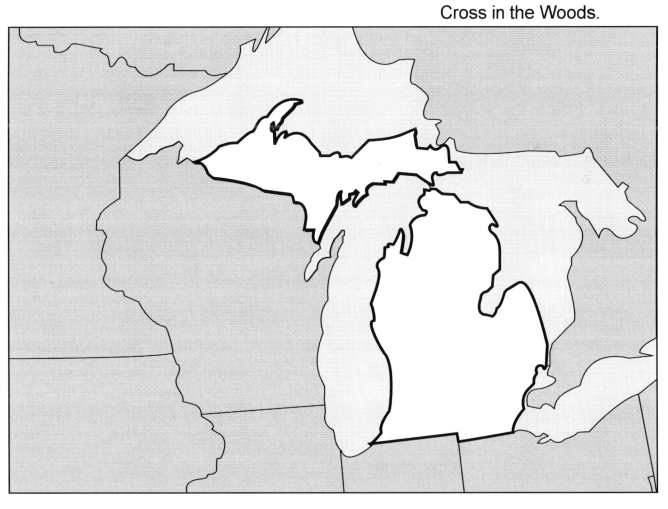

Florida

Entered the Union
March 3, 1845

Florida

Capital: Tallahassee
Population: 19,057,542
Size: 65,755 sq mi
Statehood: March 3, 1845 (27th)
Motto: In God We Trust
Nickname: The Sunshine State
Bird: Mockingbird
Flower: Orange Blossom
Tree: Sabal Palmetto
Fun Fact: Fort Lauderdale has 185 miles of local waterways and is know as the Venice of America.

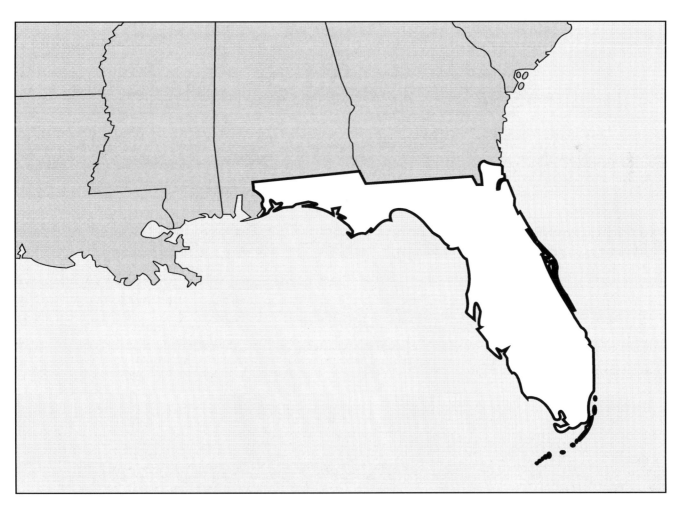

Texas

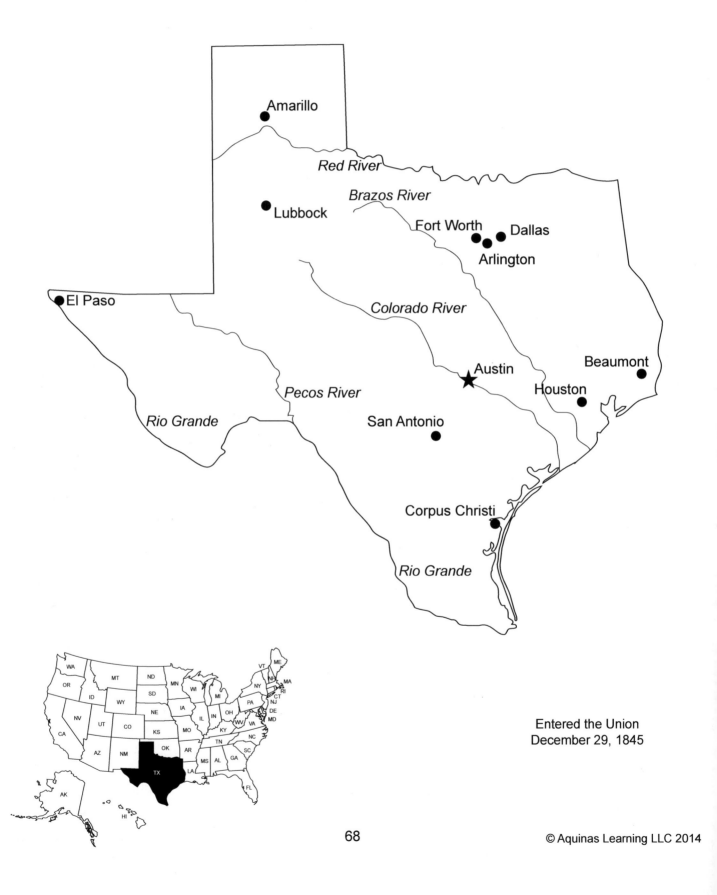

Entered the Union
December 29, 1845

Texas

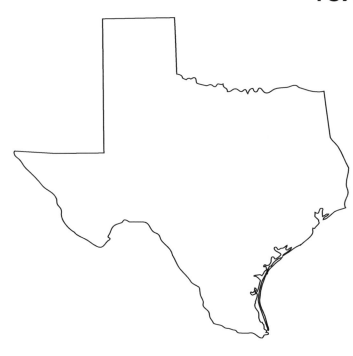

Capital: Austin
Population: 25,674,681
Size: 268,241 sq mi
Statehood: December 29, 1845 (28th)
Motto: Friendship
Nickname: The Lone Star State
Bird: Mockingbird
Flower: Bluebonnet
Tree: Pecan
Fun Fact: Texas was its own independent country from 1836 to 1845.

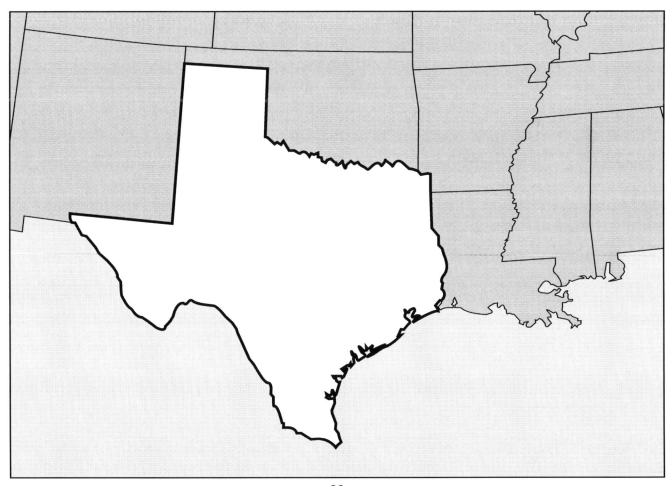

Iowa

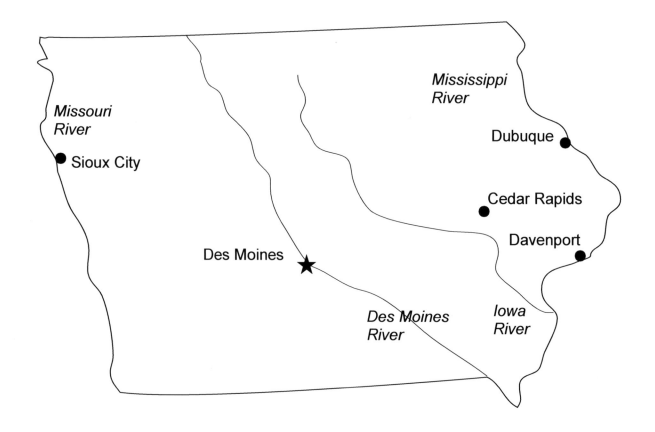

Entered the Union
December 28, 1846

Iowa

Capital:	Des Moines
Population:	3,062,309
Size:	56,272 sq mi
Statehood:	December 28, 1846 (29th)
Motto:	Our Liberties We Prize and Our Rights We Will Maintain
Nickname:	The Hawkeye State
Bird:	Eastern Goldfinch
Flower:	Wild Prairie Rose
Tree:	Oak
Fun Fact:	200 years of balloon history are chronicled at the National Balloon Museum in Indianola, Iowa.

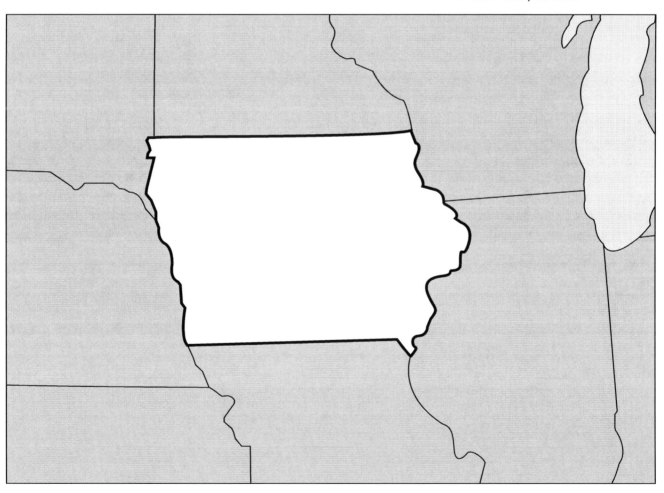

Wisconsin

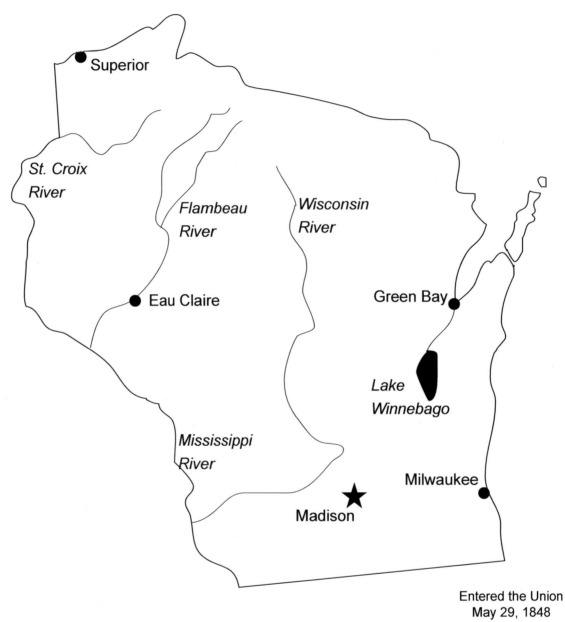

Entered the Union
May 29, 1848

Wisconsin

Capital: Madison
Population: 5,711,767
Size: 65,497 sq mi
Statehood: May 29, 1848 (30th)
Motto: Forward
Nickname: Badger State, American's Dairyland
Bird: Robin
Flower: Wood Violet
Tree: Sugar Maple
Fun Fact: More milk is produced in Wisconsin than any other states.

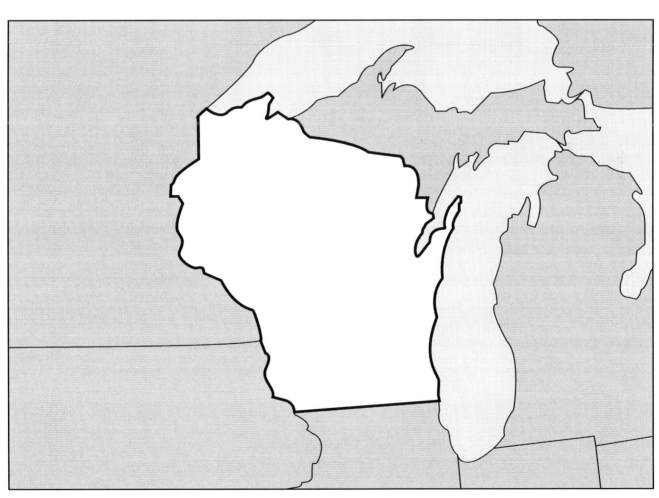

California

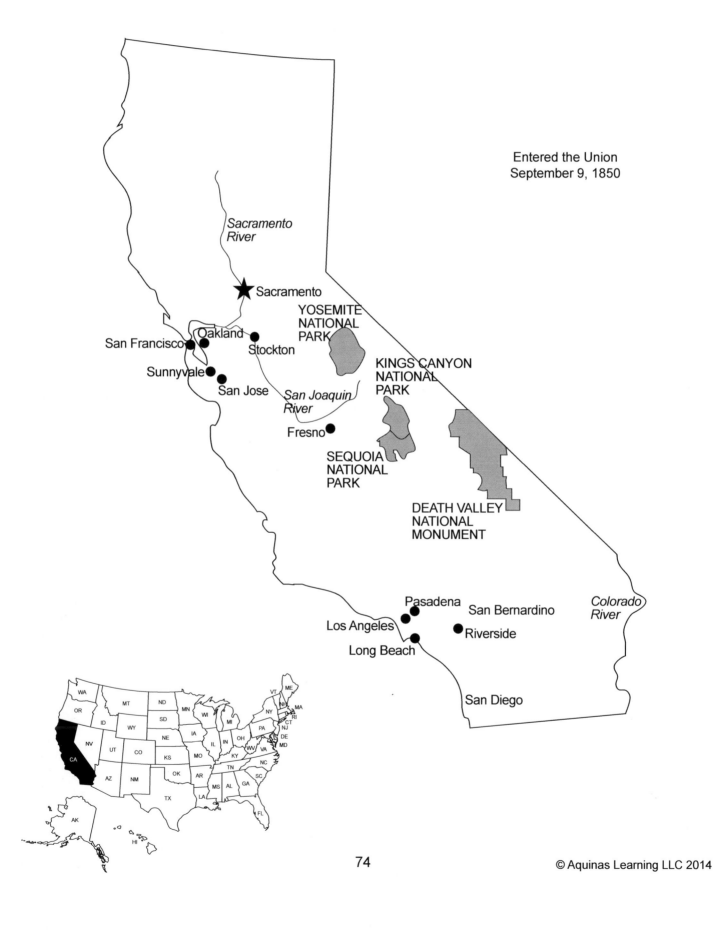

California

Capital: Sacramento
Population: 37,691,912
Size: 163,696 sq mi
Statehood: September 9, 1850 (31st)
Motto: I Have Found It
Nickname: The Golden State
Bird: California Valley Quail
Flower: Golden Poppy
Tree: California Redwood
Fun Fact: The raisin capital of the world is in Fresno, California and the Artichoke capital is Castroville.

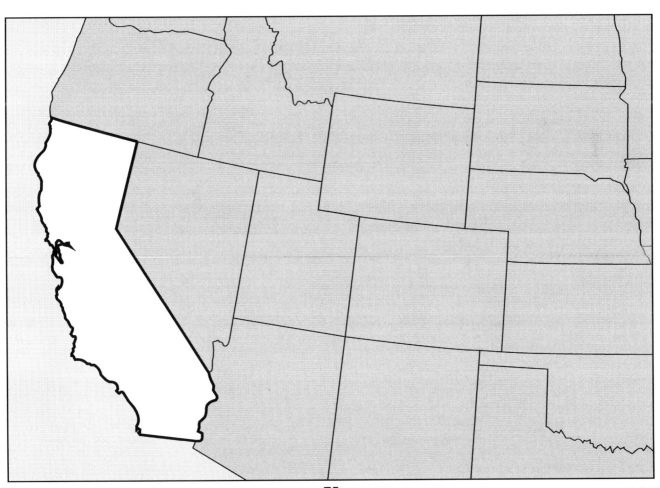

Minnesota

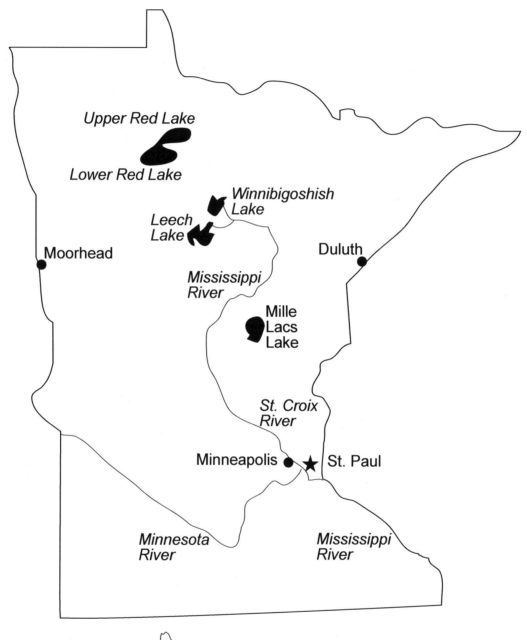

Entered the Union
May 11, 1858

Minnesota

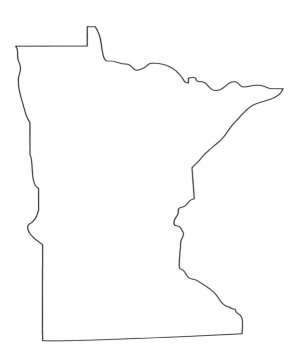

Capital: Saint Paul
Population: 5,344,861
Size: 86,939 sq mi
Statehood: May 11, 1858 (32nd)
Motto: The Star of the North
Nickname: North Star State
Bird: Common Loon
Flower: Pink and White Lady's
Tree: Red Pine
Fun Fact: Minnesota has more shoreline than California, Florida and Hawaii, combined, over 90,000 miles.

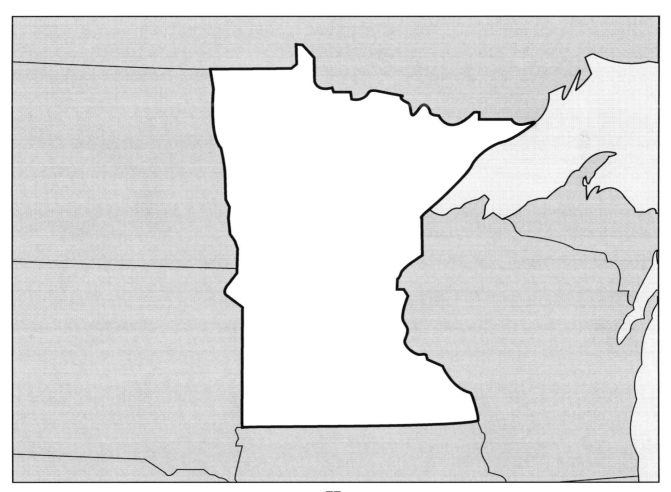

Oregon

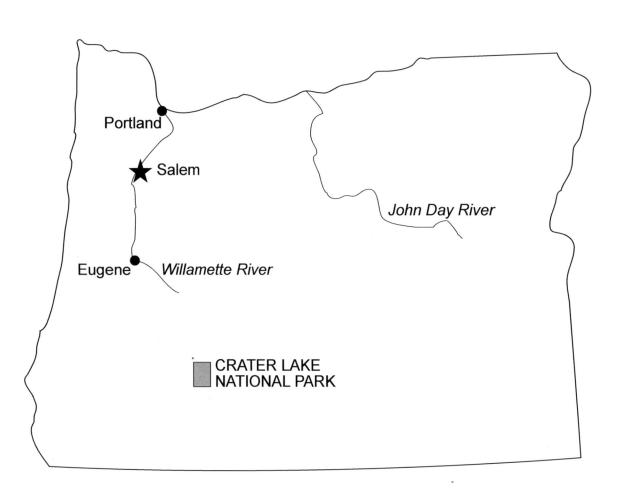

Entered the Union
February 14, 1859

Oregon

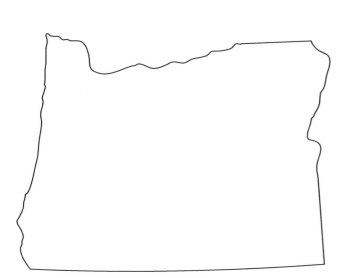

Capital:	Salem
Population:	3,871,859
Size:	98,381 sq mi
Statehood:	February 14, 1859 (33rd)
Motto:	She Flies with Her Own Wings
Nickname:	Beaver State
Bird:	Western Meadowlark
Flower:	Oregon Grape
Tree:	Douglas Fir
Fun Fact:	The deepest lake in the United States is Crater Lake, formed more than 6,500 years ago.

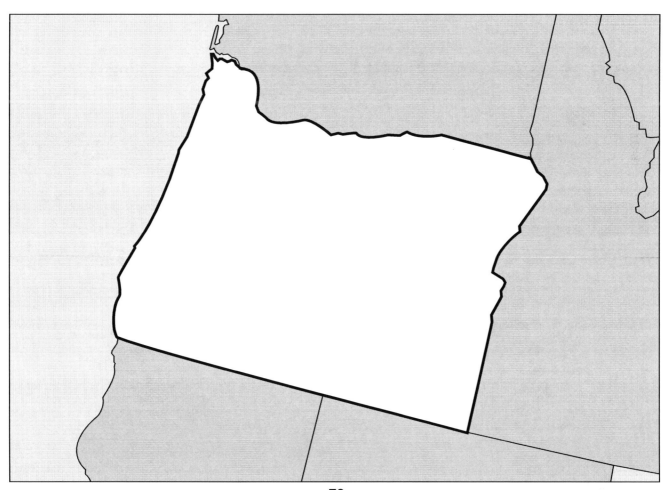

Kansas

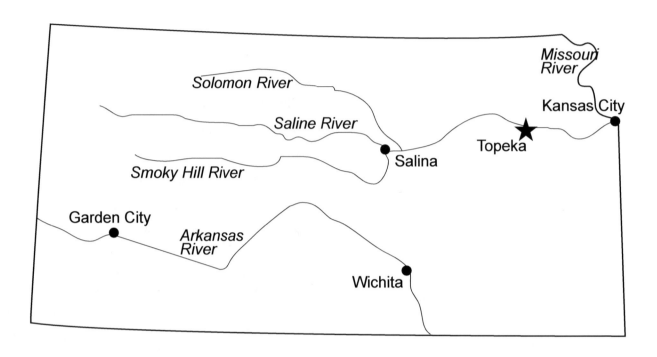

Entered the Union
January 29, 1861

Kansas

Capital:	Topeka
Population:	2,871,238
Size:	82,277 sq mi
Statehood:	January 29, 1861 (34th)
Motto:	To the Stars Through Difficulties
Nickname:	The Sunflower State
Bird:	Western Meadowlark
Flower	Sunflower
Tree:	Cottonwood
Fun Fact:	The worlds longest grain elevator is located in Hutchinson, Kansas and is over ½ mile long.

West Virginia

Entered the Union
June 20, 1863

West Virginia

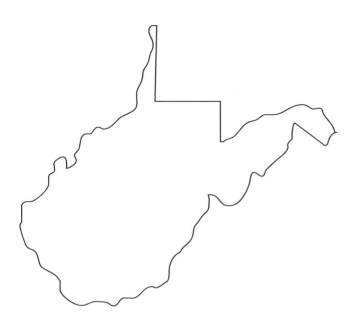

Capital:	Charleston
Population:	1,855,364
Size:	24,230 sq mi
Statehood:	June 20, 1863 (35th)
Motto:	Mountaineers Are Always Free
Nickname:	Mountain State
Bird:	Cardinal
Flower:	Big Rhododendron
Tree:	Sugar Maple
Fun Fact:	The first 4-H camp in the US was in Jackson's Mill.

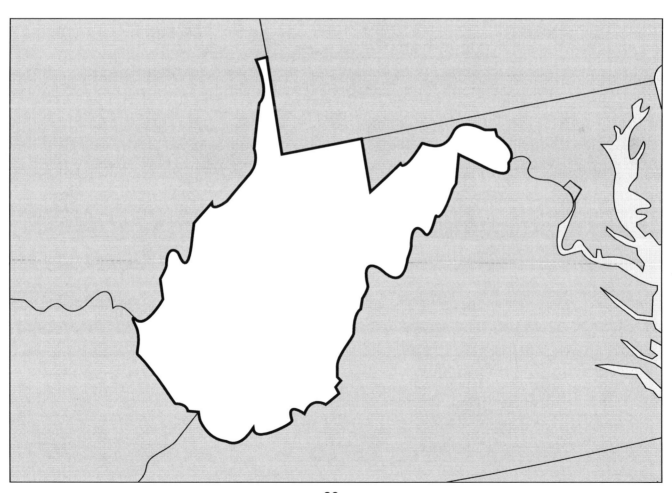

Nevada

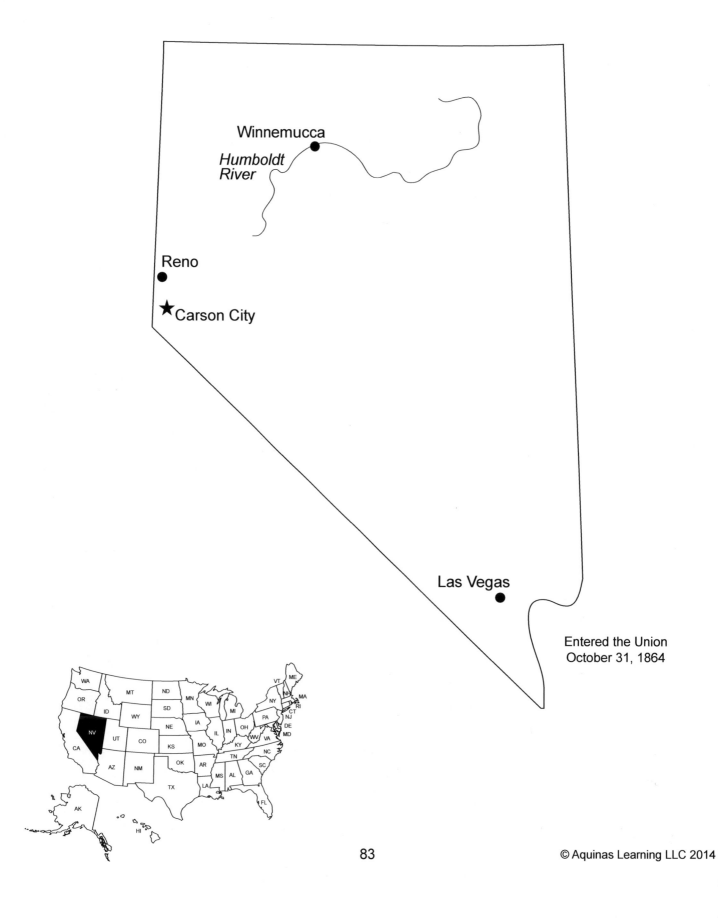

Nevada

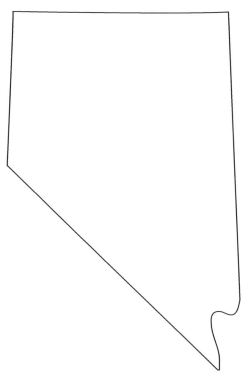

Capital: Carson City
Population: 2,723,322
Size: 119,562 sq mi
Statehood: October 31, 1864 (36th)
Motto: All For Our Country
Nickname: Silver State, The Sagebrush State
Bird: Mountain Bluebird
Flower: Sagebrush
Tree: Single Leaf Pinon and Bristlecone Pine
Fun Fact: Camels were used as pack animals up to 1870 in Nevada.

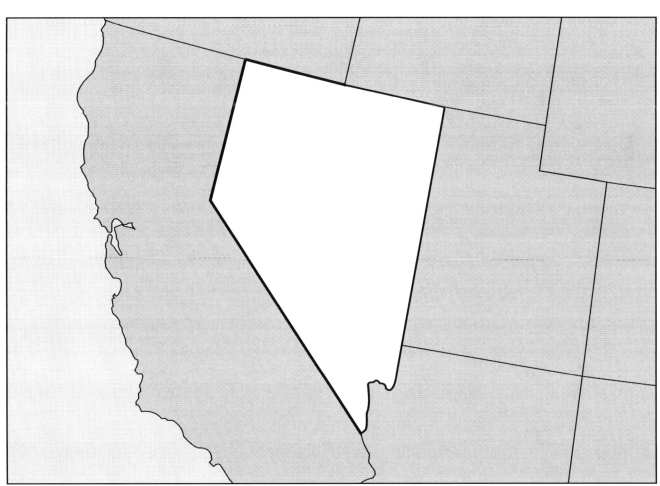

Nebraska

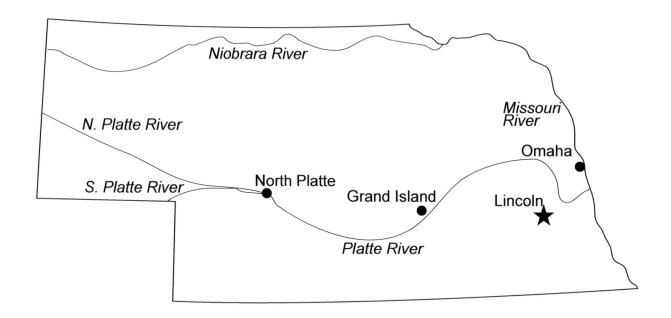

Entered the Union
March 1, 1867

Nebraska

Capital:	Lincoln
Population:	1,842,641
Size:	77,354 sq mi
Statehood:	March 1, 1867 (37th)
Motto:	Equality Before the Law
Nickname:	Cornhusker State
Bird:	Western Meadowlark
Flower:	Goldenrod
Tree:	Eastern Cottonwood
Fun Fact:	Nebraska is home to the largest porch swing in the world. It can hold 25 adults and is located in Hebron, Nebraska.

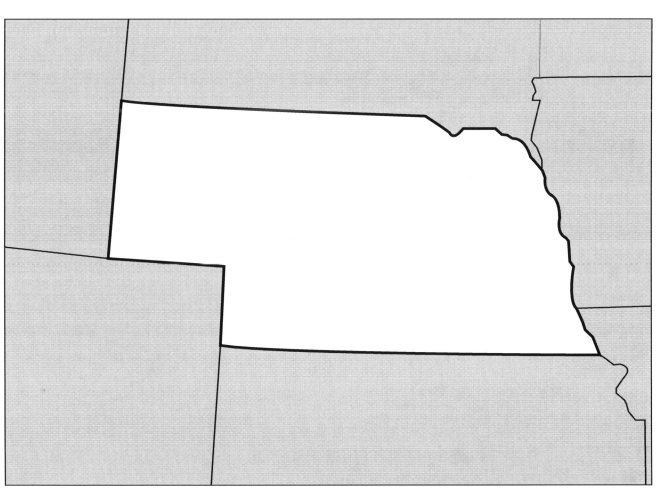

Colorado

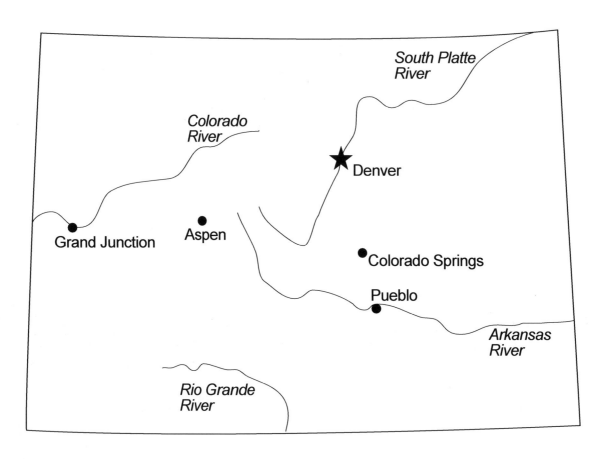

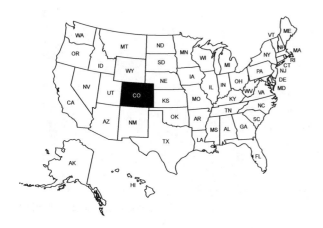

Entered the Union
August 1, 1876

Colorado

Capital:	Denver
Population:	5,116,796
Size:	104,094 sq mi
Statehood:	August 1, 1876 (38th)
Motto:	Nothing without Providence
Nickname:	The Centennial State
Bird:	Lark Bunting
Flower:	Rocky Mountain Columbine
Tree:	Colorado Blue Spruce
Fun Fact:	The largest rodeo in the world is held every year at the Western Stock show in Denver.

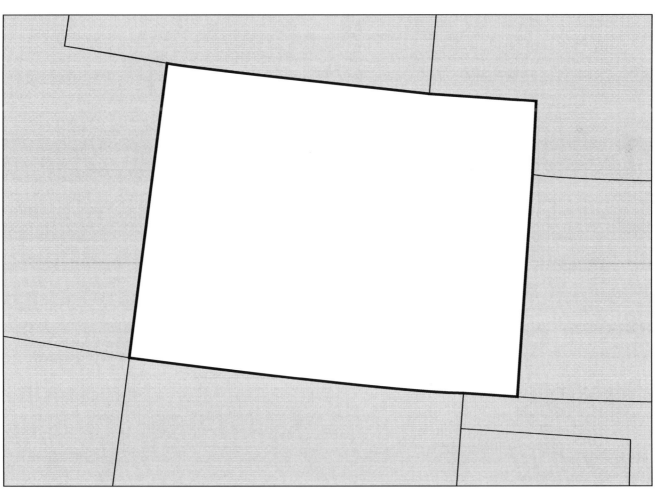

North Dakota

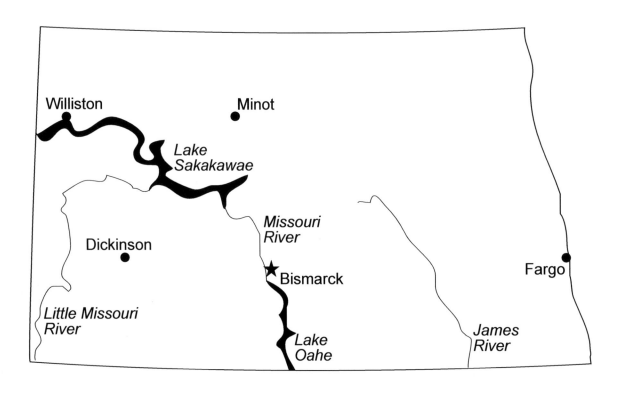

Entered the Union
November 2, 1889

North Dakota

Capital: Bismarck
Population: 683,932
Size: 70,700 sq mi
Statehood: November 2, 1889 (39th)
Motto: Liberty and Union, Now and Forever, One and Inseparable
Nickname: Peace Garden State, Roughrider State,
Bird: Western Meadowlark
Flower: Wild Prairie Rose
Tree: American Elm
Fun Fact: Frontier Village in Jamestown is home to the world's largest buffalo monument, 26 feet tall, 46 feet long and weight 60 tons.

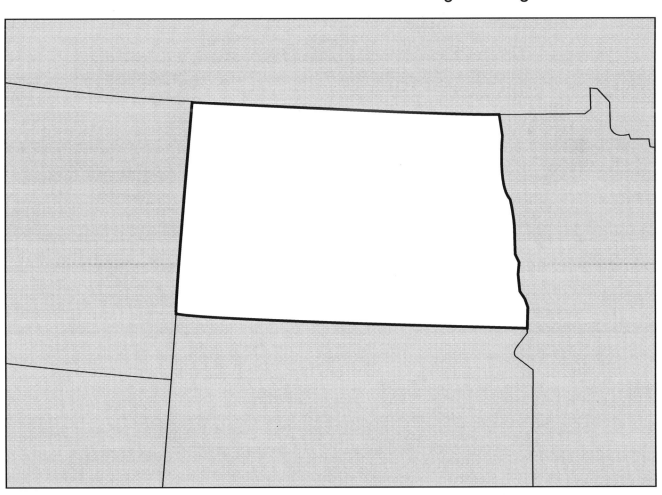

South Dakota

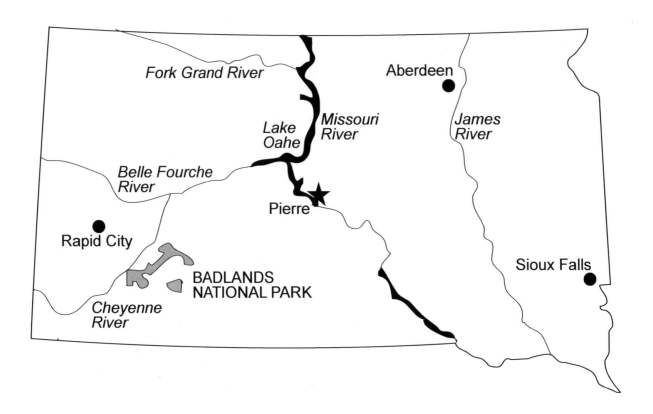

Entered the Union
November 2, 1889

South Dakota

Capital: Pierre
Population: 814,180
Size: 77,116 sq mi
Statehood: November 2, 1889 (40th)
Motto: Under God the People Rule
Nickname: Great Faces. Great Places
Bird: Ring-necked Pheasant
Flower: Pasque Flower
Tree: Black Hills Spruce
Fun Fact: The world's largest sculpture, when finished, will be the Crazy Horse Memorial in Custer County, 563 feet high.

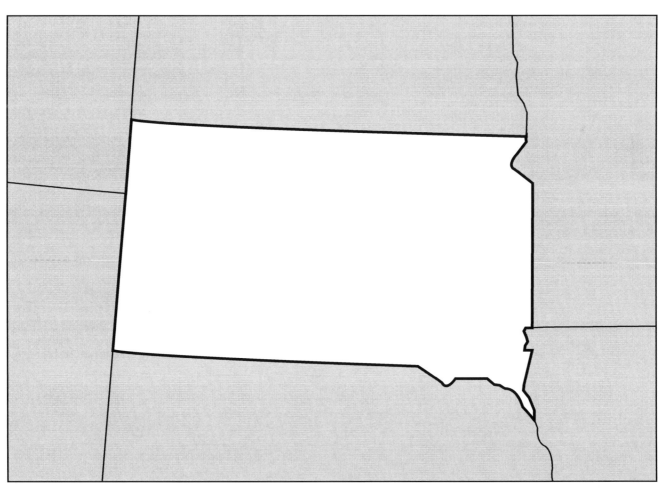

Montana

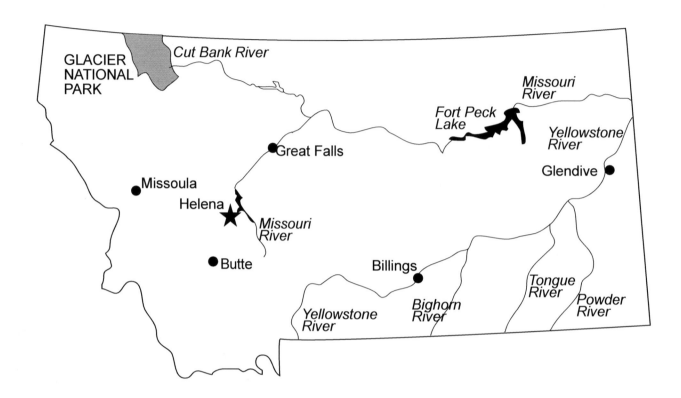

Entered the Union
November 8, 1889

Montana

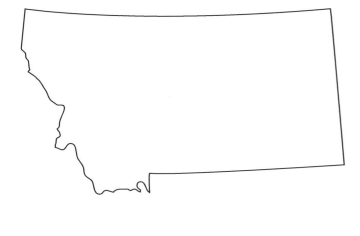

Capital: Helena
Population: 998,199
Size: 147,042 sq mi
Statehood: November 8, 1889 (41st)
Motto: Gold and Silver
Nickname: Big Sky Country, the Treasure State
Bird: Western Meadowlark
Flower: Bitterroot
Tree: Ponderosa Pine
Fun Fact: Montana has more species of mammals than any other state.

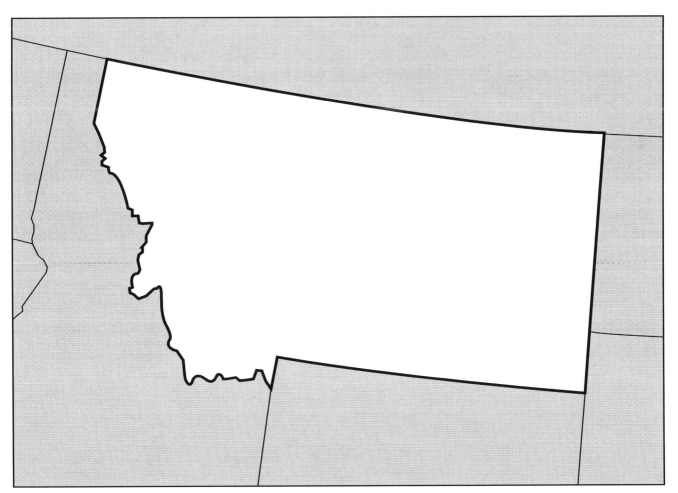

Washington

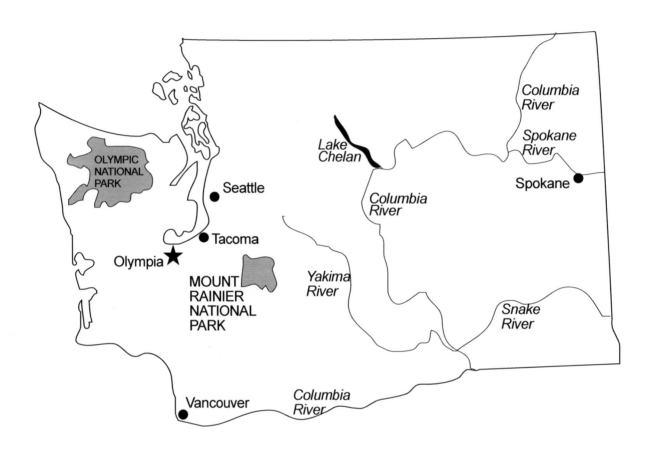

Entered the Union
November 11, 1889

Washington

Capital: Olympia
Population: 6,830,038
Size: 71,300 sq mi
Statehood: November 11, 1889 (42nd)
Motto: By and By
Nickname: The Evergreen State
Bird: Willow Goldfinch
Flower: Western Rhododendron
Tree: Western Hemlock
Fun Fact: The world's largest building, a Boeing final assemble plant, is located in Everett, Washington.

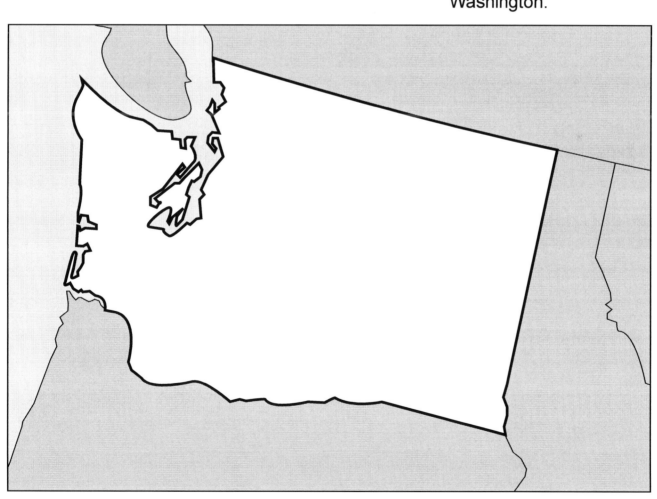

Idaho

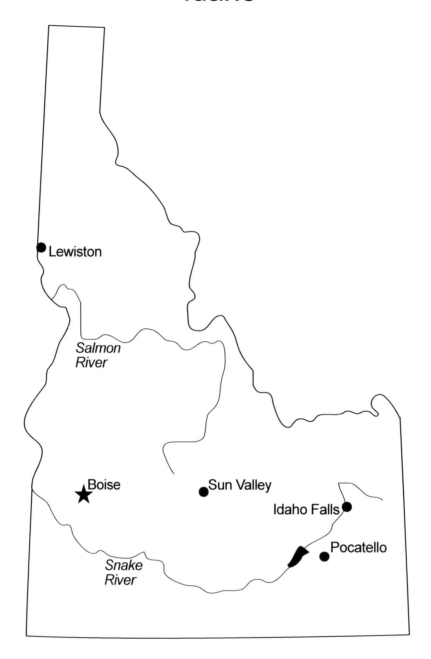

Entered the Union
July 3, 1890

Idaho

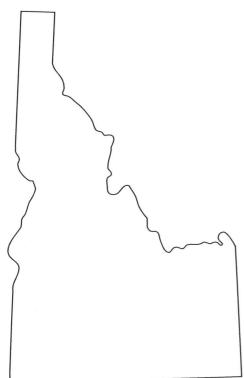

Capital:	Boise
Population:	1,584,985
Size:	83,570 sq mi
Statehood:	July 3, 1890 (43rd)
Motto:	Let it be Perpetual
Nickname:	The Gem State
Bird:	Mountain Bluebird
Flower:	Syringa – Mock Orange
Tree:	White Pine
Fun Fact:	The deepest gorge in America, Hell's Canyon, located in Idaho.

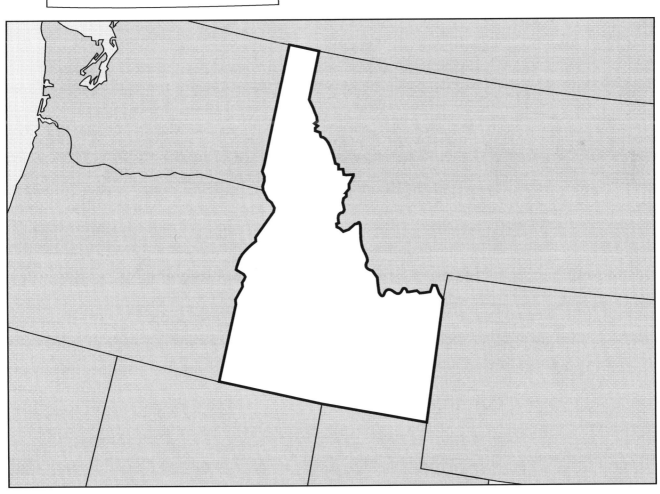

Wyoming

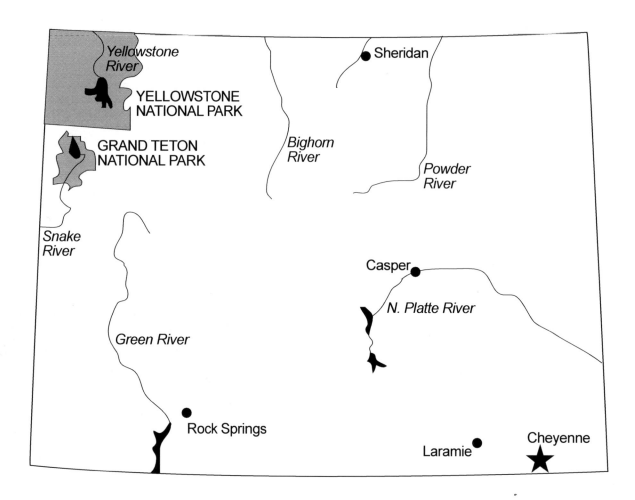

Entered the Union
July 10, 1890

Wyoming

Capital: Cheyenne
Population: 568,158
Size: 97,814 sq mi
Statehood: July 10, 1890 (44th)
Motto: Equal Rights
Nickname: Equality State, The Cowboy State
Bird: Western Meadowlark
Flower: Indian Paintbrush
Tree: Cottonwood
Fun Fact: The first official National Park was established in 1872 in Wyoming, Yellowstone National Park.

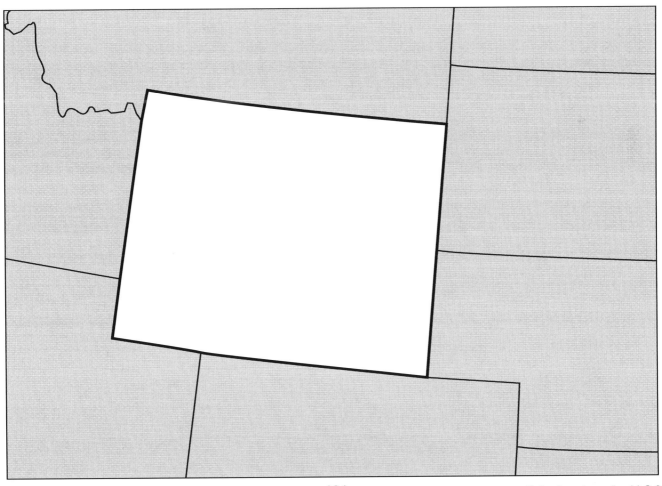

Utah

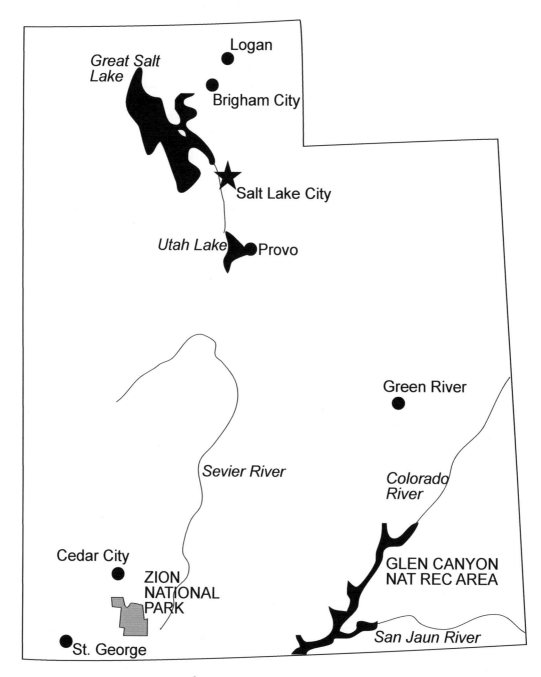

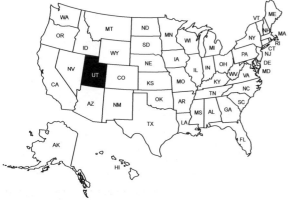

Entered the Union
January 4, 1896

Utah

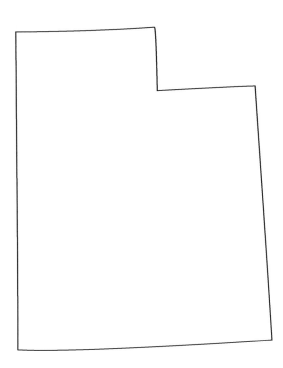

Capital: Salt Lake City
Population: 2,817,222
Size: 84,899 sq mi
Statehood: January 4, 1896 (45)
Motto: Industry
Nickname: Beehive State
Bird: American Seagull
Flower: Sego Lily
Tree: Blue Spruce
Fun Fact: The country's first department store was established in the late 1800's and is still going today.

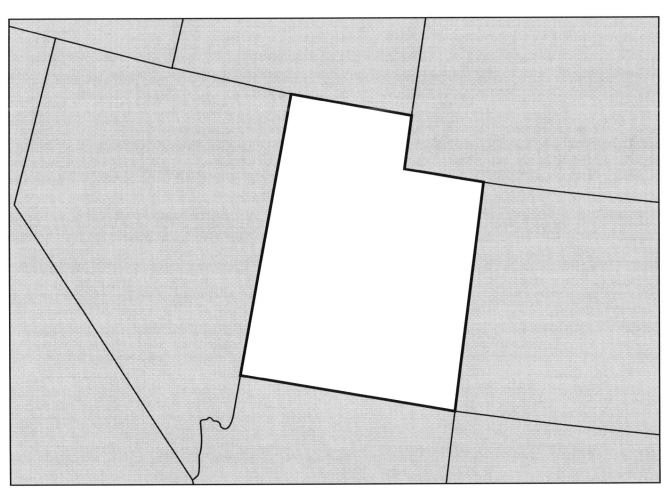

Oklahoma

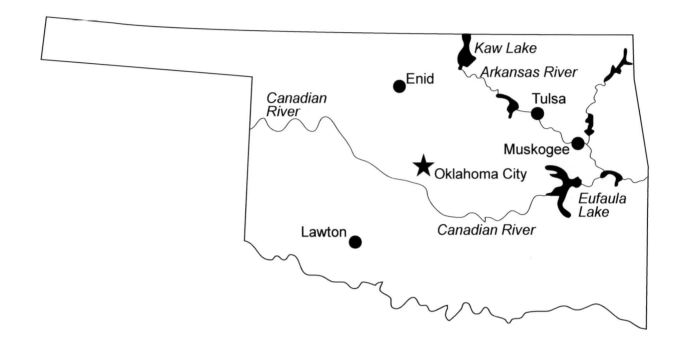

Entered the Union
November 16, 1907

Oklahoma

Capital: Oklahoma City
Population: 3,791,508
Size: 69,898 sq mi
Statehood: November 16, 1907 (46th)
Motto: Labor Conquers All Things
Nickname: The Sooner State
Bird: Scissor-tailed Flycatcher
Flower: Oklahoma Rose
Tree: Redbud
Fun Fact: Oklahoma City is the home of the National Cowboy Hall of Fame.

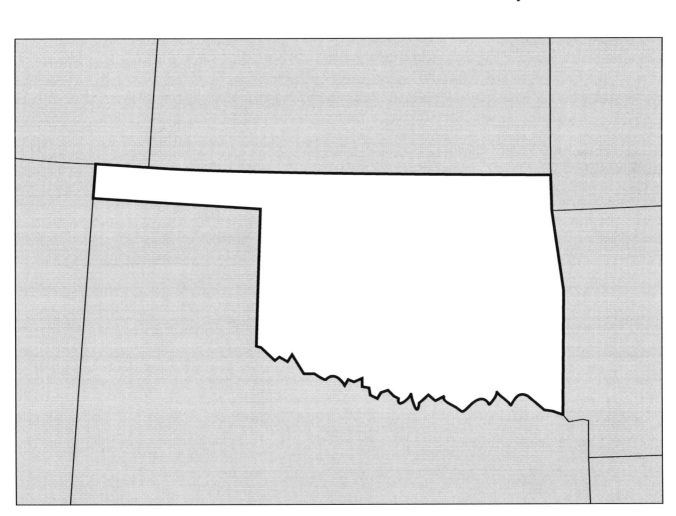

New Mexico

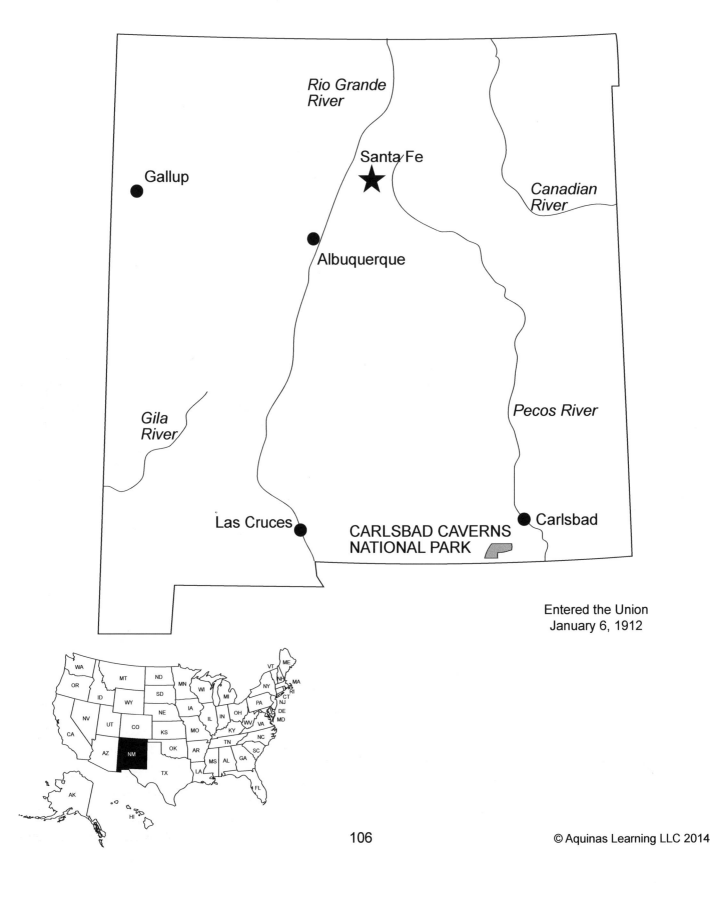

Entered the Union
January 6, 1912

New Mexico

Capital: Santa Fe
Population: 2,059,179
Size: 121,589 sq mi
Statehood: January 6, 1912 (47th)
Motto: It Grows As It Goes
Nickname: Land of Enchantment
Bird: Roadrunner
Flower: Yucca Flower
Tree: Pinon
Fun Fact: New Mexico has the highest state capital in the country, Santa Fe, at 7,000 feet above sea level.

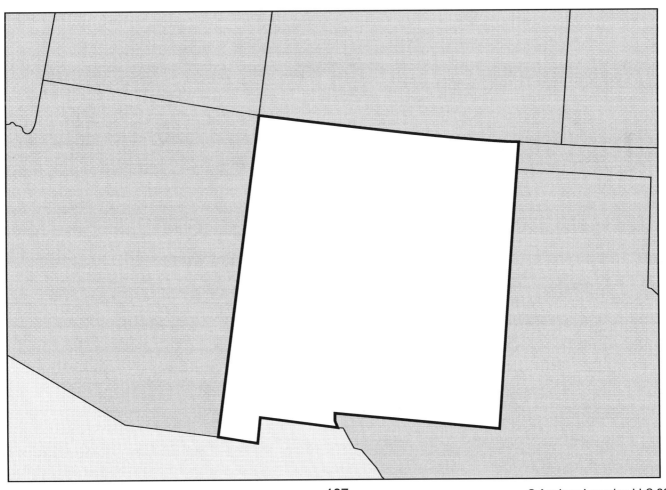

Arizona

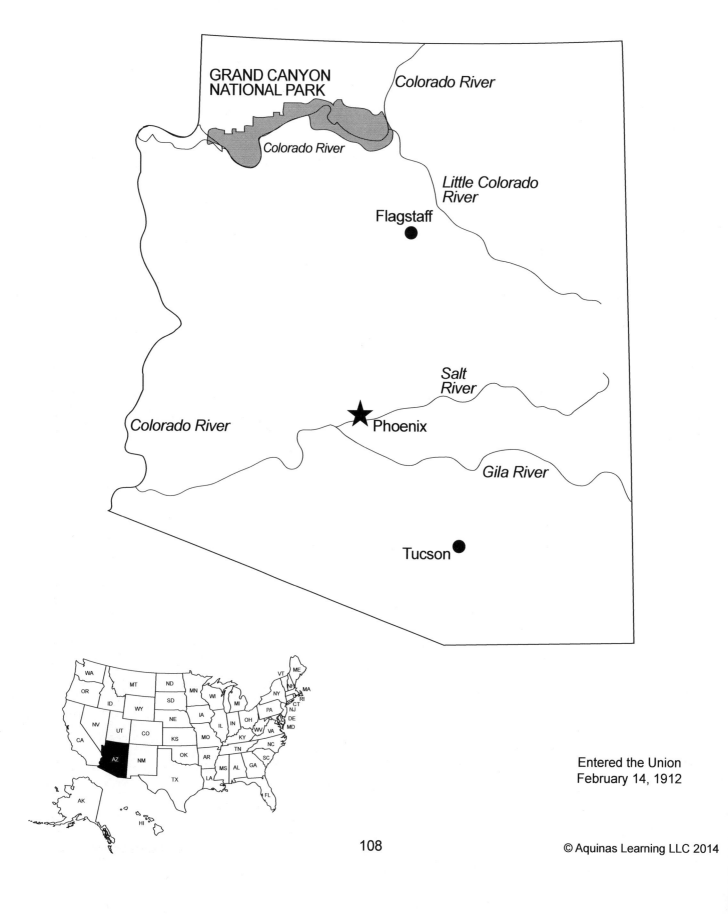

Entered the Union
February 14, 1912

Arizona

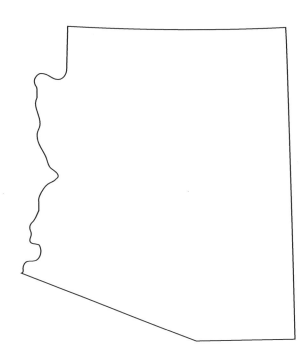

Capital: Phoenix
Population: 6,482,505
Size: 113,998 sq mi
Statehood: February 14, 1912 (48th)
Motto: God Enriches
Nickname: The Grand Canyon State
Bird: Cactus Wren
Flower: Saguaro Cactus Blossom
Tree: Palo Verde
Fun Fact: The original London bridge from London, England was shipped over stone-by-stone and reconstructed in Lake Havasu City at the London Bridge Resort.

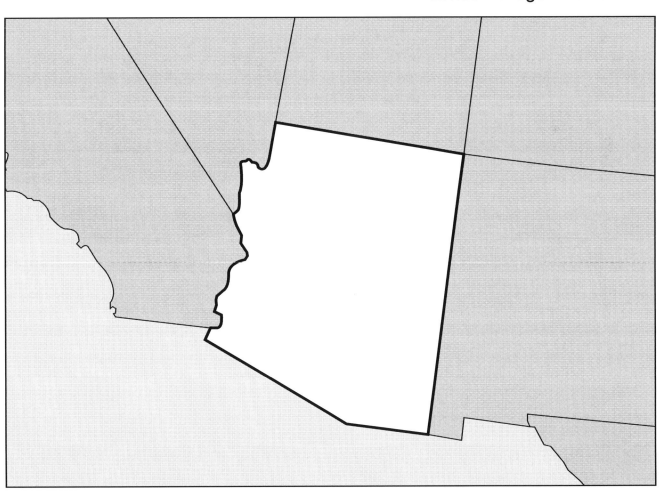

Alaska

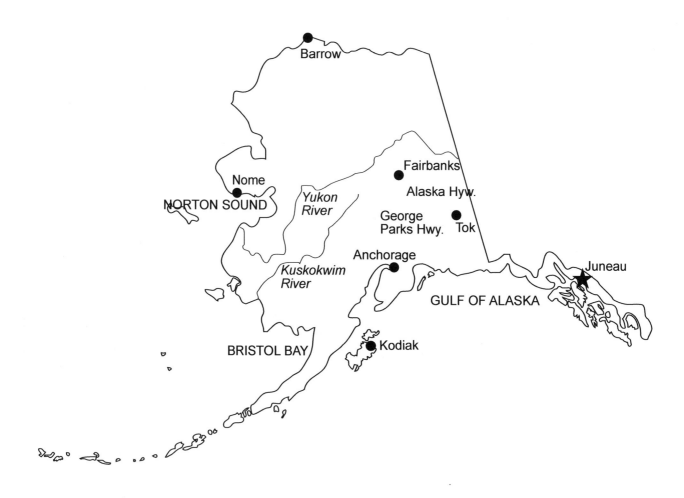

Entered the Union
January 3, 1959

Alaska

Capital: Juneau
Population: 710,231
Size: 663,268 sq mi
Statehood: January 3, 1959 (49th)
Motto: North To The Future
Nickname: The Last Frontier
Bird: Willow Ptarmigan
Flower: Forget Me Not
Tree: Sitka Spruce
Fun Fact: Alaska is so huge that if laid on top of the US map it would extend from coast to coast.

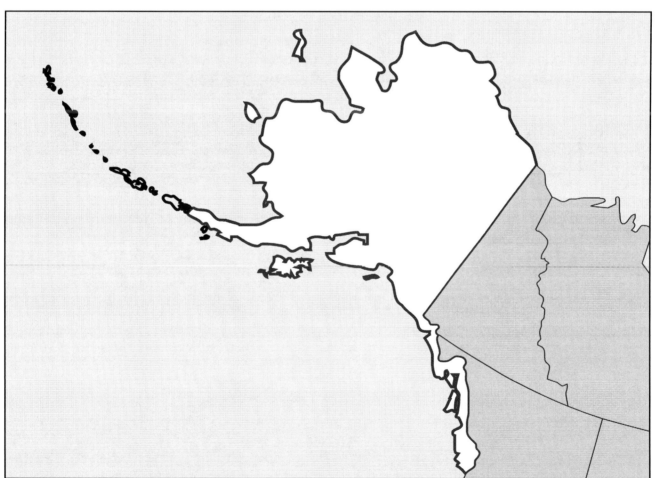

Hawaii

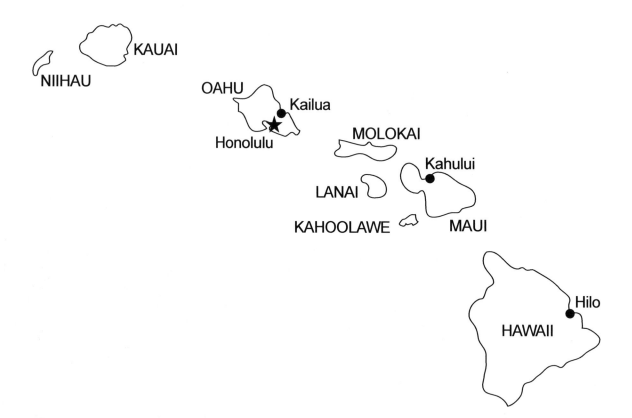

Entered the Union
August 21, 1959

Hawaii

Capital: Honolulu
Population: 1,374,810
Size: 10,931 sq mi
Statehood: August 21, 159 50th)
Motto: The life of the land is perpetuated in righteousness
Nickname: The Aloha State, The Paradise of the Pacific
Bird: Nene (Hawaiian Goose)
Flower: Pua Aloalo
Tree: Kukui - Candlenut
Fun Fact: The Hawaiian Islands are the tops of the biggest mountain range in the world.

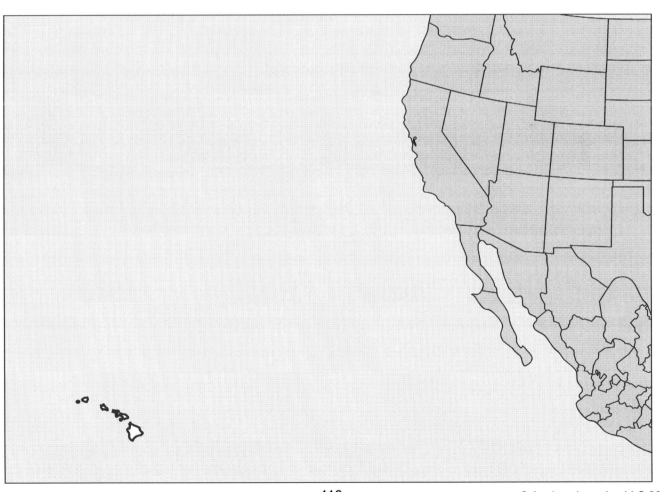

Northern Mariana Islands

- Farallon De Pajaros
- Maug Islands
- Asungion
- Agrihan
- Pagam
- Alamagan
- Guguam
- Sarigan
- Anatahan
- Farallon De Medinilla
- Tinian
- Saipan
- Aguijam
- Rota
- Guam
- Mariana Trench

Guam
- Agana

Saipan
- Garapan
- Chaian Kanoa

Northern Mariana Islands

Guam

Saipan

Puerto Rico

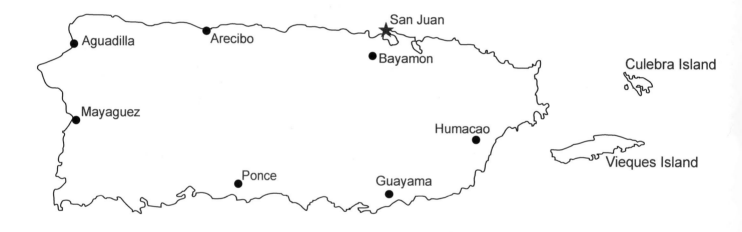

Ceded to the Union
December 10, 1898

Puerto Rico

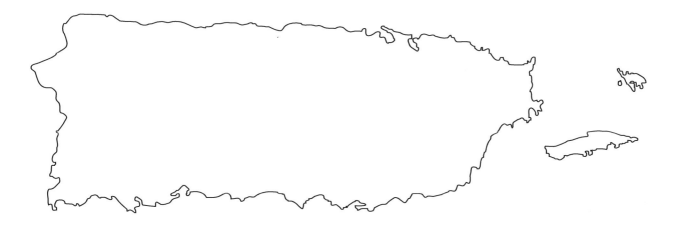

United States Virgin Islands

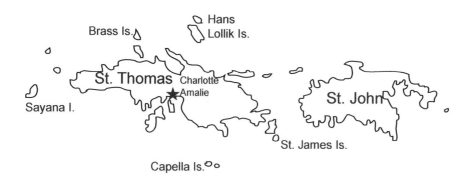

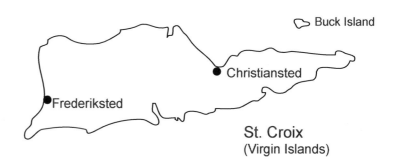

US Takes Possession
March 31, 1917

United States Virgin Islands

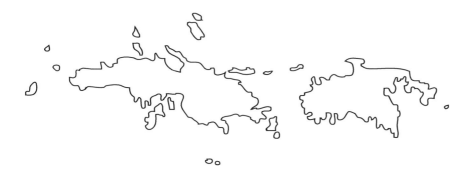

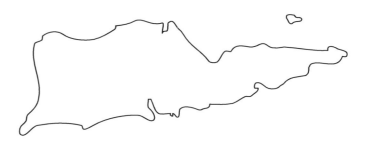

About the Aquinas Learning Program

Aquinas Learning is a classical Catholic mentoring program whereby students meet once a week to learn key facts in core subjects; learn skills from coaching and modeling; develop virtuous habits; and discuss ideas from the "great conversation" passed down through the generations. These pursuits train the students' wills and cultivate their minds enabling them to grow in wisdom and virtue.

As home-educators, we have come to know the value in providing for the day-to-day education of our children and how much effort is involved in planning for such an education. Using our Three-Cycle Curriculum framework spanning from Kindergarten to 6th grade allows parents more time to teach lessons rather than plan them.

By studying the history, literature, art, music, and great ideas of Western civilization, we strive to develop love for learning (speaking, writing, listening, thinking) and contemplating God through the appreciation of what is True, Good, and Beautiful. Aquinas Learning partners with parents, God's stewards of their children, in raising them to know, love, and serve God in this world in order to gain eternal happiness with Him in the next.

www.AquinasLearning.com

About J. Bruce Jones, Map Designer

J. Bruce Jones is a Massachusetts based business graphic designer, software developer, musician and independent video producer. Bruce works with corporate and non-profit clients in his design business. He also writes on a variety of topics including, playing and learning music with his essential chord books, video guides to help get found on YouTube, how to manuals for working with Powerpoint and the World of Maps editable maps, and various books and articles on business and marketing.

Bruce is the developer of the World of Maps editable clip art map collection for PowerPoint and Adobe Illustrator for presentations, illustrations, graphic design, education and websites. Distributed through various websites including; www.mapsfordesign.com, www.bjdesign.com and Amazon. He is also the developer of Antique and Historical Maps, a collection of royalty free, antique digital maps from 1500s to the 1900s, used for graphic design, illustration, web sites and education.

Bruce is very active in both producing and creating original programming for local public access television and the web and also for businesses interested in promoting themselves using video.

www.BruceJonesDesign.com
www.MapsForDesign.com
www.BJDesign.com

Made in the USA
Las Vegas, NV
30 November 2020